Overcoming
Your Child's Fear of Dogs

Overcoming Your Child's Fear of Dogs

A Step-by-Step Guide for Parents

Stefani M. Cohen, LCSW
with contributions from Cathy Malkin, MA

This book was written with the intent to provide information for parents to help their child overcome the fear of dogs. It is paramount that all interactions between children and dogs be supervised. The information presented in this book is for educational purposes and presented to the best of my knowledge. It is not designed to replace a professional diagnosis or professional treatment. The author has provided general information and cannot make any assurances in regard to the applicability of any information with regard to any person or circumstance. The author shall have no liability or responsibility for any such action taken or decision made by the reader of this book and no liability for any loss, injury, damage or impairment allegedly arising from the information provided in this book.

Overcoming Your Child's Fear of Dogs: A Step-by-Step Guide for Parents

Published by Gatekeeper Press
2167 Stringtown Rd, Suite 109
Columbus, OH 43123-2989
www.GatekeeperPress.com

Back Cover Photos by Susan Woog Wagner Photography and Venture Photography
Illustrations by Jenn Kay, Jenn's Doodle World

ISBN (paperback): 9781662900198

Dedication

This book is dedicated to my grandchildren who remind me daily how magical it is to share your life with a dog.

Contents

Acknowledgments

This book truly took a village. My method for helping children overcome their fear of dogs has been living in my head for decades and I'm thrilled that it's finally out there for people to use. I want to thank my husband, Gerry, for taking a leap of faith many years ago and agreeing to open our family up to having dogs. My daughter, Becky, helped me see what it's like to be petrified around dogs and how important it is to overcome the fear. My son Rich showed me that rough and tumble kids can also be gentle and compassionate with dogs. My sister, Cathy Malkin, has shared her wealth of knowledge about dogs with me and has been my cheerleader throughout this whole process. Andrea Deierlein sat with me patiently for hours and hours while we got the information into a readable format. Leah Moore deserves a shout out for her confidence in me and the importance of the topic. Jenn Inashvili with her artistic flair made Fozzie come alive in her illustrations and truly captured his fun-loving personality.

Lastly, I want to thank all the brave children willing to face their fear of dogs and their families for allowing me to help them learn to enjoy dogs and feel safe around them.

Introduction

"I learned that courage was not the absence of fear, but the triumph over it. The brave man is not he who does not feel afraid, but he who conquers that fear."

—Nelson Mandela

"I think dogs are the most amazing creatures; they give unconditional love."
—Gilda Radner

Author's note: This book is designed to be a guide for parents, but therapists will find it useful as well. While it is meant for children ages five to twelve, it can be helpful for anyone afraid of dogs, including adults. The format uses exposure therapy, which is a method for overcoming many fears that I have tailored specifically to the fear of dogs, known as cynophobia. Throughout the book, I refer to children as "they," unless I specifically know their gender.

Welcome to this book on **Overcoming Your Child's Fear of Dogs - A Step-by-Step Guide for Parents**. I have combined my personal and professional experience to create this guide. There is little information out there to help kids who are afraid of dogs, so I felt compelled to put something together to help other parents. I know firsthand how difficult it is when your child is afraid of dogs. It not only impacts their emotional development but also daily life and family dynamics. As a parent, I lived through the same emotions and challenges that you are experiencing. When my daughter Becky was afraid of dogs, I felt frustrated because I didn't understand why she was afraid. Her fear became a stressor for our family life. One of my motivations to write this book was to write it from a parent's perspective, in addition to my perspective as a therapist and dog lover.

My work as a therapist and parenting consultant has brought me in contact with many cases of childhood anxiety. I know that when a child is anxious, it affects the entire family. Parents often tell me that they feel worried and anxious about whether or not they will encounter a dog because they know how much it terrifies their child. As a parenting counselor, I realized that you can't help kids overcome fear without their parents' support. Parents need to understand what fear is, where it comes from, and how to overcome it.

The fear of dogs is also known as cynophobia and is an anxiety disorder.

Fear of dogs is more common than most people realize, and in today's world it is virtually impossible to avoid dogs. About ten percent of kids have phobias or significant fears, and animal phobias are the most common. If you're afraid of spiders or bees, you can usually avoid direct contact with them. However, it is more difficult to avoid dogs as compared to other animals because they are everywhere. Kids who are scared of dogs will go to great lengths to avoid them.

My goal is to support, educate, and empower kids to better understand dogs. I want children to feel safe around dogs so they can face their fears and hopefully end up establishing a relationship with a dog. In this book, I will introduce several strategies that teach children to take back the leash, quite literally. They will learn not to be overpowered by fear, but instead how to be in control of the situation.

Overcoming Your Child's Fear of Dogs will help you better understand your child's fear and why it's so important to help them overcome it. My method was developed based on my knowledge of child development and anxiety in children. While I am very familiar with dogs and their behavior, I am not an official dog trainer.

There is much to be gained in helping your child overcome their fear of dogs. Children who overcome this fear gain self-confidence, a feeling of empowerment, and resilience. With this book, you will learn how you can best support your child and how to use exposure therapy to desensitize your child to their fear. You will learn tools and techniques to help your child replace fear with knowledge. I include anecdotes (names have been changed) from my practice as well as a case study to illustrate how best to use the Overcoming the Fear of Dogs Protocol (OFOD) that I developed.

The OFOD Protocol is an easy-to-follow ten-step program based on exposure therapy. It uses a hierarchy of exercises that gradually increases your child's comfort around a dog. My method involves using a real dog that has been vetted thoroughly for reliability and tolerance around children. This book gives suggestions on how to go about finding such a dog and handler. There are two chapters designed specifically to teach parents and children about the body language of dogs and how dogs communicate. The final chapter explores the human-animal bond and the benefits of interacting with dogs.

I am very grateful that my work has led me to combine my passion for helping children with my love for animals. As a humane educator, I teach respect and kindness for all living beings as well as dog-bite prevention and general safety around dogs. As an animal lover, I have been able to work side by side with my canine partners. Fozzie, a ten-year-old male Keeshond, has assisted in helping many kids overcome their fear of dogs.

Fozzie Cohen

Fozzie's breed — Keeshond — is affectionately
known as the "Smiling Dutchman."

Stefani M. Cohen, LCSW
March 2020

Chapter 1:

About Fear And Phobias

"To escape fear, you have to go through it, not around."
—Richie Norton,
author of *The Power of
Starting Something Stupid*

In this section, we will explore how normal childhood fears can develop into more significant problems, and how a child's strong fear of dogs can affect the lives of their family members. We will see how this plays out in the stories of real children and their families. (Names have been changed.) Topics covered in this section include:

❑ Fear in General
❑ How Fear of Dogs Develops
❑ How Being Afraid of Dogs Impacts Your Child's Life
❑ Behavioral and Emotional Symptoms of Being Afraid
❑ Why You Should Help Your Child Overcome Their Fear of Dogs

> **Fear is a universal feeling, often accompanied by physical discomfort, that is an emotional response to a threat that may be real or perceived.**

Fear is part of being human. It is a mechanism that has helped the human race survive. A healthy dose of fear keeps us safe and out of harm's way. For example, most people will be fearful or at least uncomfortable during a turbulent airplane flight or if they think that their house has been burglarized. Others may feel nervous when they walk on a bridge. We stand back on the platform when a train approaches to keep ourselves safe. And, if we're honest, a healthy dose of caution around dogs is also important.

Similarly, most people feel afraid when they encounter a dog that displays aggressive or threatening behavior. This is a natural reaction, and it is common sense to use a certain amount of caution around dogs. According to the Centers for Disease Control, there are almost five million dog bites every year in the United States.

This kind of fearful reaction is fleeting and usually does not require treatment. Someone who is frightened by a dog behaving aggressively isn't necessarily going to be afraid when they encounter a dog walking calmly on a leash or playing in a backyard. But sometimes people develop a strong fear of dogs, which can turn into a phobia. This is known as *cynophobia.*

A phobia is a form of anxiety disorder characterized by an intense fear of an object or a situation in which an object may appear. These fears are usually irrational and are often accompanied by physical symptoms such as shortness of breath, nausea, diarrhea, and even full-blown panic attacks.

General Development of Fear in Children

Typical childhood fears include stranger anxiety for infants and separation anxiety for toddlers. From the ages of four to six, children are often afraid of things based in their imagination, such as ghosts and monsters. Kids aged seven to twelve are typically afraid of things they hear about on the news or things happening around them. They may hear about wildfires, school shootings, divorce, and other occurrences. Adults also have fears, which might include fear of heights, fear of public speaking, or fear of flying.

Please know that throughout a child's development, fears and anxieties will come and go. This is very natural and normal. Parents need to remember that fears are common in childhood. As parents, we tend to worry about anything and everything, but most kids outgrow their fears as they get older and more mature. Occasionally, however, a specific fear can deepen to the point where it has a significant impact on the child's daily life. Being afraid of dogs can fall into this category.

Many children will be cautious or timid when they first encounter a dog, but with encouragement and guidance will quickly learn that dogs can be fun to pet. It is important to teach children how to interact safely and respectfully with dogs. Chapters Six and Seven will provide further insight and practical advice on this topic.

> **Remember:**
> **We tend to be afraid of things we don't understand or things we feel we can't control. For many children, dogs fall into this category.**

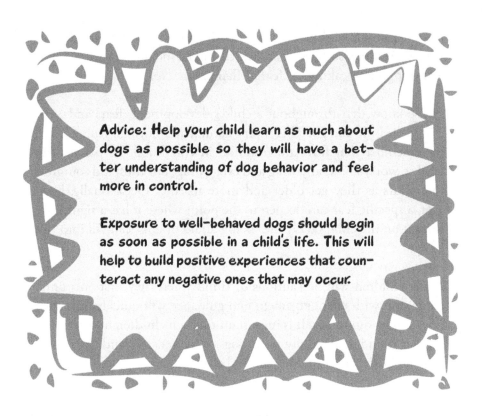

Advice: Help your child learn as much about dogs as possible so they will have a better understanding of dog behavior and feel more in control.

Exposure to well-behaved dogs should begin as soon as possible in a child's life. This will help to build positive experiences that counteract any negative ones that may occur.

Children have unique personalities, and it's not uncommon for siblings to react differently to dogs. My grandchildren have had consistent, supervised interactions with my dog Fozzie since they were infants. When my grandson Oliver was a baby, he startled easily; he would cry if someone sneezed or spoke loudly. At first, he cried whenever Fozzie barked, but eventually he got used to the barking. Now he and Fozzie are good friends. Oliver's younger brother Sam was less cautious than Oliver had been at the same age. Sam was less sensitive to loud noises such as barking, and he often sought out Fozzie to play. Juliette, my youngest grandchild, showed interest and was curious about Fozzie from early on. When he barks, she scrunches her face and looks startled but recovers quickly when we all say "yay!" And then she claps. These examples illustrate how a child's innate temperament can affect how they see and react to the world.

Physical Symptoms of Fear

When a child is afraid of dogs, you are likely to see one or more of the following symptoms. These symptoms can occur whether a child is in direct contact with a dog or is just anticipating contact with a dog in the future.

- ❑ Sweaty hands
- ❑ Rapid heartbeat
- ❑ Nausea or other stomach ailments
- ❑ Headaches
- ❑ Irritability or emotional fragility, such as crying or having a tantrum with little provocation

Abigail's Story, Age Seven

Abigail started sleeping poorly a few weeks before Easter. Her appetite decreased and she was crying a lot for no real reason, according to her parents. After a week of these behavioral changes, her mother did some exploring with her, and Abigail was able to say that she was worried about going to her Aunt Tara's house for Easter because Tara had two dogs.

It turned out that Abigail had become hesitant around dogs after her best friend was bitten by one. Abigail's mother contacted me for help and we did a few sessions utilizing my Overcoming Fear of Dogs Protocol (OFOD – Chapter Five outlines this method in detail).

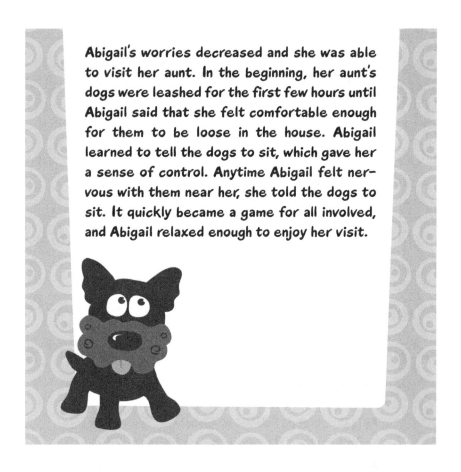

Abigail's worries decreased and she was able to visit her aunt. In the beginning, her aunt's dogs were leashed for the first few hours until Abigail said that she felt comfortable enough for them to be loose in the house. Abigail learned to tell the dogs to sit, which gave her a sense of control. Anytime Abigail felt nervous with them near her, she told the dogs to sit. It quickly became a game for all involved, and Abigail relaxed enough to enjoy her visit.

Some children can't even look at a dog without panicking. Others can be near a dog as long as the dog doesn't come too close. These feelings can range from mild to debilitating. It is important to accept that the child is afraid and to address that fear in a supportive manner rather than trying to talk them out of it.

We can support the child by using exposure therapy (Chapter Five will discuss this in depth) to desensitize them. Using this technique will reduce their anxious responses and replace them with knowledge and a plan.

Given the prevalence of dogs in households in the U.S.[1], it is unlikely that anyone can go through life avoiding dogs completely. Complicating this is the fact that most dog owners underestimate the fear some children have when it comes to their pet dogs. They see their dog as friendly and adorable and can't understand why someone would be afraid of their beloved pets. Many of my clients have described experiences in which a dog's owner said the dog was friendly or liked children, but the animal knocked them over, licked, or even bit the child. This is why it is important to **understand** your child's fear of dogs, to follow the steps outlined in this book, and, if necessary, to seek the help of an additional adult or professional.

We need to empower children to feel confident and secure around dogs. This starts with learning how to interact safely with dogs. The truth is that all dogs *can* bite. When first encountering a dog, it is important to always ask the owner's permission to pet the dog. Some dogs are afraid of children or don't feel comfortable around them. We also need to teach children about specific times when dogs are more likely to act aggressively and when it's best to stay away from them. For example, a mama dog that is nursing her pups may react aggressively to an intrusion; a dog that is in a car may feel territorial, and a dog that is hurt may bite out of self-preservation.

How Parents Can Help Their Children Overcome Their Fear of Dogs

- ❑ Recognize your own feelings about dogs. If you feel fearful or uneasy around dogs, seek help from another adult who is more confident around them.
- ❑ If possible, arrange for your child to observe or interact with registered therapy dogs, especially in the early stages of your desensitization work. Therapy dogs are specially trained to be gentle, calm, and comfortable with strangers. Places to find therapy dogs that are accessible to the public include library programs. You can contact a local chapter of Pet Partners, Therapy Dogs International, or the American Kennel Club to find out where they are doing visits and how your child

can participate. Dogs who have received their Canine Good Citizen (CGC) from the American Kennel Club are good candidates for this as well.

❑ Understand and accept your child's fear. Get as much information as possible by talking with your child about their specific concerns so you can adapt your work to address them. For example, if your child is afraid of being licked by a dog, manage the dog so that it doesn't lick your child.

❑ Educate yourself and your child about dog behavior and safety around dogs.

❑ Look at pictures and videos of dogs and puppies interacting appropriately with children. Always view these by yourself first so you do not inadvertently play a video of an aggressive dog in front of your child.

❑ Interact with dependable dogs and respectful owners.

❑ Be a good role model by acting relaxed and happy around dogs. If you feel nervous around dogs, try not to show it.

❑ Observe dogs from a distance.

❑ **Most importantly, resist the urge to get a dog in hopes that this will help your child get over their fear. This almost always backfires.**

How the Fear of Dogs Develops

Being fearful is a natural part of childhood, and a healthy dose of caution helps to keep us safe. Chapter Six discusses safety around dogs, which will help your child understand what makes dogs tick and guide them on how to interact with dogs.

Fears develop in four different ways.

1. By having a personality and temperament prone to developing fears.
2. By having a direct negative personal experience.
3. By observing someone having a negative experience.
4. By hearing about or being taught about negative experiences.

Personality-Type Experience

Through my work with children and families, I have identified a **personality-type experience,** which refers to fears that develop primarily because of specific personality traits. In general, kids who are naturally prone to developing strong fears tend to be cautious, observant, and sensitive.

Dogs are unpredictable and may feel foreign to some children. This can create fear and anxiety in children because they don't understand why a dog is acting a certain way. They also don't know how to control the dog or their own feelings. This can lead to the child feeling out of control, anxious, helpless, and scared. In my experience, these children tend to be sensitive and very observant of their environment. Teaching children that dogs are like them can help dogs seem less strange, and therefore less intimidating. For example, dogs need food, water, exercise, shelter, toys, and love. So do children! Dogs also have feelings, and some are even afraid of children.

Becky's Story, Age Five

To the best of our knowledge, my daughter Becky had never had a direct negative experience involving a dog, nor did she see someone else have a bad experience. In our family, we always talk about how wonderful dogs — and all animals — are. Despite this, Becky became petrified of dogs.

In Becky's case, her fear of dogs stemmed from her own temperament. Becky was observant, sensitive, and a little more anxious
than the average kindergartner. Becky had several other fears as
well, such as a fear of costumed characters, people with accents,
and the dark. She also had a wonderful imagination. This combination of characteristics made her more vulnerable than other children to developing strong fears tied to specific objects, animals,
people, or situations. Although she wasn't afraid of her grandmother's dog, which she'd known all her life, the thought of interacting with any other dogs sent her into a panic and she'd refuse
to visit the home of anyone who had a dog.

Becky could never articulate exactly what it was about dogs
that scared her, despite my best efforts. But once we helped
her to recognize her fear and began working with her using
the Overcoming Fear of Dogs Protocol described in Chapter
Five, Becky was able to manage her fear and interact with calm
and well-behaved dogs. Knowing that she could always ask the
adults to prevent a dog from approaching her helped her gradually gain confidence around them and Becky eventually learned
to love dogs.

Direct Experience

An upsetting **direct experience** would include something happening to you that made you feel uncomfortable such as a dog jumping up on you, licking you, or biting you.

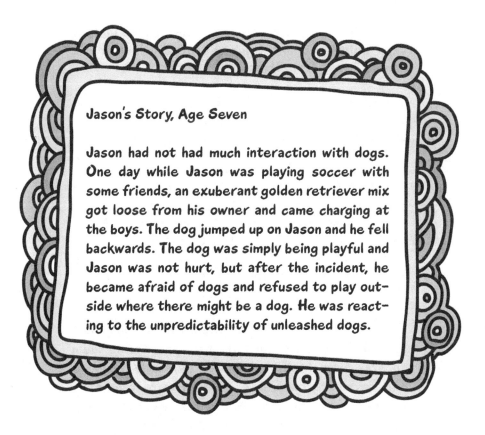

Jason's Story, Age Seven

Jason had not had much interaction with dogs. One day while Jason was playing soccer with some friends, an exuberant golden retriever mix got loose from his owner and came charging at the boys. The dog jumped up on Jason and he fell backwards. The dog was simply being playful and Jason was not hurt, but after the incident, he became afraid of dogs and refused to play outside where there might be a dog. He was reacting to the unpredictability of unleashed dogs.

Observational Experience

An **observational experience** involves your child **seeing** someone else have a negative experience or acting afraid near a dog. For example, in Jason's case, one of his friends might have become afraid of dogs from observing Jason being tackled, although, to the best of my knowledge, this did not occur. But something similar did happen to Marie.

Marie's Story, Age Six

Marie and her brother Michael (age eight) visited their neighbor who had just adopted a terrier mix named Pansy from the animal shelter.

Unfortunately, the adults did not supervise the children's interactions with the new dog. Michael and his friend began to run and chase the dog. After a few minutes of this, the boys cornered Pansy, and although the boys' intentions were playful, the dog felt frightened and thought the only way to stop them was to bite. The dog bit Michael's leg. Fortunately, the bite did not penetrate Michael's clothing and no medical treatment was needed. The adults immediately put Pansy on a leash, and after that incident, they took care to supervise the dog's interactions with children.

They also took Pansy to obedience training and helped the children learn when she was telling them to stay away from her through her body language and warning growls. The children were taught to interact more respectfully and safely with the dog. These efforts helped ensure that Pansy never bit any child again. Interestingly, Michael never felt afraid of Pansy or any other dogs after his experience. However, his sister Marie became very afraid of dogs after witnessing the dog bite. My professional assessment of her fear characterized it as severe.

Instructional Experience

An **instructional experience** can generate a fear of dogs as well. This can include seeing a video or movie with an aggressive dog or even being told by your grandmother over and over to "be careful around dogs — they can bite you." The experience of Juan fits into this category.

Juan's Story, Age Nine

Juan's grandmother was raised in Puerto Rico, where there were many stray dogs. She had been bitten once and had observed several other people being bitten during the 45 years that she lived there. For as long as Juan could remember, his abuela had been telling him to stay away from dogs, in much the same way that she would warn him to stay away from a hot stove. His fears became problematic when his parents and two sisters began talking about getting a family pet. I worked with both Juan and his grandmother to help them become more comfortable around dogs and learn how to interact safely with them. Little by little, their feelings about dogs changed, and I am happy to report that the family adopted an older small dog from a shelter and they were all able to live peacefully under one roof.

Pria's Story, Age Four

Pria is the niece of a client of mine. She was afraid of dogs, and no one could figure out why. After previewing this book, my client realized that her niece was most likely afraid because the girl's mother was allergic to dogs. Pria's mother would often say things like "I can't go to _____ because there's a dog there." Pria interpreted this to mean that dogs are dangerous. Once my client figured this out, Pria's family spoke to her and explained that Mommy wasn't afraid of dogs, they just made her sneeze. Pria's father then made a concerted effort to expose Pria gradually to friendly dogs, and her fear dissipated quickly.

Not all children learn to love dogs as Becky did, and some develop a behavior called the approach/avoidance coping mechanism.

The Approach/Avoidance Coping Mechanism

Some children have a strong desire to interact with dogs but are prevented from doing so by their fear of them. This combination is called approach/avoidance. These children can often be motivated by rewards and praise, which helps to magnify the desire to approach and override the impulse to avoid.

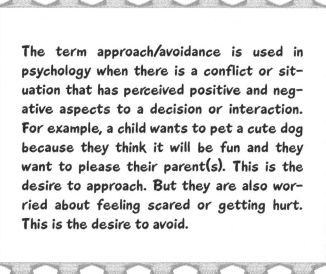

The term approach/avoidance is used in psychology when there is a conflict or situation that has perceived positive and negative aspects to a decision or interaction. For example, a child wants to pet a cute dog because they think it will be fun and they want to please their parent(s). This is the desire to approach. But they are also worried about feeling scared or getting hurt. This is the desire to avoid.

A protective measure against developing cynophobia is early and frequent exposure to friendly and well-behaved dogs. This worked well for Michael, who, as described in the story above, did not develop a fear of dogs even after being bitten by one. He had a strong foundation of many positive interactions with dogs. However, as we know, this is not a guarantee.

My own sister Cathy was bitten by a dog in early childhood but never developed a fear of them. When she was still a toddler, she pulled our dog's tail while he was eating and he bit her. Our mother found a new home for the dog and later adopted a child-friendly dog. From that day forward, every dog we had (and there were many) enjoyed its meals away from children. Developing a strong foundation of enjoyable experiences with dogs can help insulate your child from becoming afraid of them, even if they experience difficult interactions with dogs at some point.

With all fears, it is helpful to understand how and why your child became affected by it. Here are some questions that will help you understand your child's fear of dogs.

- ❑ When did your child start to be afraid of dogs?
- ❑ Did something happen directly to your child? (Direct experience)
- ❑ Did your child see someone else have a bad experience with a dog? (Observational experience)
- ❑ Has your child gotten a message that dogs are dangerous? (Instructional experience)
- ❑ Does your child's sensitive nature make him or her prone to anxiety and fears? (Personality-type experience)

No matter how your child's fear of dogs developed, it's very important to address it as soon as possible. The next chapter will help you begin to do just that.

In this chapter, we saw how fears develop and the devastating effect they can have on children and their families. The next chapter will help you understand more specifically about your child's fear of dogs.

Chapter 2:
Cynophobia

"We came to see Stefani and Fozzie at a time when our daughter's fear of dogs had been escalating to the point of near panic attacks. We had tried everything we knew how to help her with this fear and knew we needed more help, because her fear had turned into cynophobia."
—Stacey W., Tarrytown, NY

If your child has a strong fear of dogs, it is important to address it as soon as possible. The more children avoid dogs, the more fearful they become of them. The fear takes up residence in their head and often gets worse as they think about all the things that scare them about dogs. It is important to support your child so they can safely face their fear of dogs. Dogs are an integral part of life in many families, and it is difficult to avoid them altogether. When your child is afraid of dogs, it can impact daily life and create tension.

These are typical questions that occur in the homes of children who are afraid of dogs:

-Will there be a dog at the bus stop?
-Is the neighbor's dog going to "escape" and run over here again?
-Is Uncle David bringing his dog to the summer beach house?
-My friend got a puppy. Do I still have to go on the playdate?

When you have a child who is petrified of dogs, it often becomes a source of conflict for family members and can seriously impact everyday life. In my case, it created daily stress and frustration when every playdate, trip to the park, walk outside, or social occasion needed to factor in whether or not we might see a dog.

Cynophobia is the medical term for an intense fear of dogs. It comes from the Greek words for dog (kyon) and fear (phobos). In the Diagnostic and Statistical Manual of Mental Disorders 5th Edition (DSMV), published by the American Psychiatric Association, cynophobia is classified as a specific phobia under the general category of animal phobias.

Lance's Story, Age Ten

Lance had been able to manage his fear of dogs by not going to the homes of friends who had dogs. He would also scout the playground for dogs before he would get out of the car. If he saw a dog, he would insist that his mother let him stay in the car. I would classify Lance's fears as having a moderate impact on his life.

One year, several weeks before Thanksgiving, Lance's Aunt Sharon adopted a small Pomeranian dog. Scruffy was energetic, vocal, and friendly, but not yet well-trained. Lance's family had always spent Thanksgiving at Aunt Sharon's house, and Lance began to have nightmares and long crying jags due to his anticipatory anxiety about having to interact with the new dog.

Lance's parents began to argue about whether or not the family was going to go to Sharon's house for Thanksgiving. Lance's mother wanted to stay home because Lance was so worried about meeting Scruffy. Lance's father didn't understand why Lance was afraid of dogs and tried to talk Lance into going to his aunt's house by saying he would buy him a new skateboard. The conflict between his parents escalated into yelling. Lance became even more upset because he felt he was causing the disagreement between his parents.

In Lance's case, we utilized his desire to go to his aunt's home for Thanksgiving to jump-start his exposure therapy. (Exposure therapy will be explained in Chapter Five.) Lance understood that if he participated fully in our sessions and knew what to expect from Scruffy, he would eventually feel better.

When I met Lance and completed an assessment, he was able to articulate that he was afraid of dogs because they were loud and jumpy. At the same time, he said he wanted desperately to be able to go to his aunt's home for Thanksgiving and to make his parents stop yelling, because he felt responsible for their arguments.

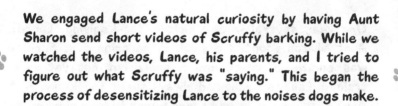

We engaged Lance's natural curiosity by having Aunt Sharon send short videos of Scruffy barking. While we watched the videos, Lance, his parents, and I tried to figure out what Scruffy was "saying." This began the process of desensitizing Lance to the noises dogs make.

In addition, Fozzie and I worked with Lance to help him feel in control around dogs. Because Fozzie does not jump up on people and is well trained for sit, stay, and down, Lance was able to put Fozzie through his paces and see that he was safe around Fozzie. Because Scruffy was young and just beginning his obedience training, it was not realistic to expect that Scruffy wouldn't jump up on Lance, so the adults needed to be vigilant in prohibiting this behavior. Since Aunt Sharon lived more than two hours away, it was not practical to involve Scruffy directly in our exposure therapy sessions. We used FaceTime to have virtual interactions with Scruffy.

As illustrated by Lance's story, intense fear of dogs can impact a child's whole world and can cause serious issues within a family. For most people who have cynophobia, fear and anxiety are triggered by the sight of dogs. But for some, like Lance, the mere thought of a dog is enough to trigger these feelings. This is known as anticipatory anxiety.

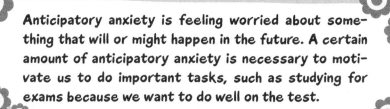

Anticipatory anxiety is feeling worried about something that will or might happen in the future. A certain amount of anticipatory anxiety is necessary to motivate us to do important tasks, such as studying for exams because we want to do well on the test.

As you will see throughout this book, most kids cannot be talked out of their fears. **They need to have brief, positive experiences with dogs in order to feel safe and in control around them**. I helped Lance understand that dogs bark as their way of talking. If you listen carefully, you will hear dogs making all kinds of sounds. For example, my dog Fozzie has a special bark to alert me when someone is at the door, a whiny bark to ask for more treats, and a "hello" bark to greet familiar people when they arrive.

Fozzie says: Remember that it's important for kids to feel safe and in control. Parents need to understand that their children's fears are real and should be respected.

It's key to give your child permission to ask for what they need. For example, it is absolutely okay for kids to ask that dogs not jump on them or greet them over-enthusiastically. When you walk into a home that has an out-of-control dog, you can and should ask that the dog be leashed and/or controlled. Dogs need to be trained to be respectful towards children and adults. Just as we expect children to say "please" and "thank you," we should expect that a dog will not jump up on us or knock us over.

How Cynophobia Affects Family and Social Dynamics

When your child is afraid of dogs, it can have a significant impact on family life. Lance's parents disagreed on how to help Lance. It almost came down to the difficult choice of whether or not to celebrate a holiday with extended family. The parents' relationship was significantly strained as a result of Lance's fear of dogs.

Sibling relationships can also become strained.

Ava and Julia's Story, Eight-Year-Old Twins

Ava loved all animals, especially dogs, and nagged her parents daily for a dog. Julia, on the other hand, was so fearful of dogs that the mere possibility of seeing one sent her into tears. The two girls argued about it constantly, and the non-fearful twin would tease her sister about being a scaredy-cat. Their parents were unsure how to handle this; they tried to defend Julia, but their patience with the situation ultimately ran out. My work with this family using my counseling background helped the girls improve their relationship.

After a little psychological digging, it became clear that both girls felt jealous of the other. Ava was jealous that Julia seemed to get a lot of attention when she expressed her fear of dogs. She was also angry that Julia stood in the way of getting a family pet. Julia was upset and hurt when Ava teased her. It took a few sessions to clear the air. Then I assigned Ava the job of 'role model' to demonstrate for Julia how to pet Fozzie and how to get him to do some obedience tricks.

Julia's resistance and fear decreased when she saw her sister interact safely with the dog. Shortly after we finished our sessions, the family adopted two guinea pigs — one for each girl. Guinea pigs are among my favorite small pets. They are easy to care for (if you don't mind cleaning a cage) and are very responsive when you play with them. The family contacted me a few years later to announce that they had adopted a dog from an animal shelter. The dog was calm and came with some basic training, and things were going very well.

There are endless scenarios illustrating how a child's social life can be hampered by their fear of dogs. Henry, age eight, had major meltdowns involving long crying jags before every soccer practice and game. This was because spectators often brought dogs to the field. Fearful children often refuse to go on sleepovers or playdates if there will be a dog in the house. I have stood at bus stops with fearful children helping them to interact or just stand quietly when their friends brought dogs with them. More and more places of work, and even some schools, are allowing dogs. Organizations that train service dogs, such as Guiding Eyes for the Blind, visit schools and scout groups, and children who are afraid of dogs may not be able to participate fully and may feel embarrassed about it.

Spectrum of Fear

A child's fear of dogs can range from mild to severe. It can also fluctuate depending on the situation and the particular dog.

Mild fear might look like this: Your child is fine being around grandma's older, small dog and feels okay being at the park if the dogs are leashed, but they are afraid of a friend's jumpy golden retriever puppy and might not want to visit that family because of it.

Moderate fear might include your child refusing to go on playdates unless the dogs are put in a back room.

Severe fear might manifest itself as your child feeling so afraid that they will scream and run into the road to avoid a dog being walked on the sidewalk. In addition, there may be a wide range of physical symptoms related to this level of fear. Your child might even enter full panic mode with heart palpitations, trouble breathing, crying, and screaming.

> Note: When working with your child, it is helpful to have a general sense of their temperament and a basic knowledge of how to help anxious children. Are they generally a "go with the flow" kid or do they tend to be anxious?

While it is important to pin down your child's level of fear, my approach is the same for all levels. What may vary, however, are the length of treatment and duration of sessions. It will most likely take longer to help a child with a severe fear of dogs than one who has a milder fear.

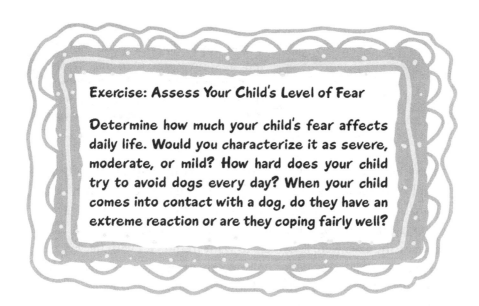

Criteria to Help Determine Whether Your Child Has a Phobia

According to Paul Foxman[2], Ph.D., author of *The Clinician's Guide to Anxiety Disorders in Kids and Teens*, the following criteria must be met for the diagnosis of a phobia:

- ❑ *An immediate fear or anxiety in response to a specific object or situation* (for our purposes, this would be a dog).
- ❑ *The phobic object or situation is either avoided or endured with intense fear or anxiety.*
- ❑ *The fear or anxiety is out of proportion to the actual danger posed by the object or situation.*
- ❑ *The pattern of fear or anxiety has lasted for at least six months.*
- ❑ *In children, crying, tantrums, freezing, or clinging may express their anxiety.*

Fozzie says: Begin to address the fear as soon as you recognize it. The more entrenched the fear becomes, the harder it can be to overcome.

In my experience, children who are afraid of dogs are usually not afraid of other animals. If they do have fears associated with other animals, these feelings are usually milder. Ruby, age nine, was afraid of both cats and dogs, but she was able to manage her fear of cats more easily. Cats were less likely to want to interact with her because she gave a clear message by ignoring them or moving away if they came near her. Unless a dog is leashed or knows how to "stay," it is very difficult to keep a dog from trying to say hello or from moving around their home and territory.

Questionnaire

(A copy of this form can be found in the Resource Section.)

The following questions will help you explore your child's level of fear and identify the specific situations that your child finds most difficult. Before beginning any kind of therapy with dogs, do an honest assessment of **your own** feelings and thoughts about dogs. This process will help you determine whether your child is picking up on overt or subtle messages about dogs from family/friends.

1. When did your child's fear of dogs begin?
2. Did your child have a specific negative experience with a dog?
3. Did your child see someone else have a specific negative experience with a dog?
4. Did your child hear about something involving a dog that happened to someone else?
5. Does your child observe you or another trusted adult being nervous around dogs?

6. Did your child develop a strong fear of dogs without an obvious triggering event or cause?
7. Does your child have other fears? Anxiety?
8. Does your child want to overcome their fear? If so, how motivated are they?
9. Would you classify your child's fear as mild, moderate, or severe?

General questions about your child:

❑ How would you describe your child's personality?
❑ Are they outgoing or reserved?
❑ Do they ask a lot of questions? Do they have a vivid imagination?
❑ Are they highly observant and/or extra cautious?

Examples of common specific fears involving dogs include:

❑ Being licked
❑ Being jumped on
❑ Being chased
❑ Being bitten
❑ The size of the dog
❑ Barking

Some children are more afraid of big dogs than smaller dogs. Other children aren't affected by differences in a dog's size but feel afraid when a dog looks at them. Some children don't want to see a dog's teeth. Barking can also provoke fear in some children. The more information you can gather, the better.

Here are two examples of specific dog behaviors that triggered a significant fear of dogs:

1. John, age eleven, was worried about being jumped on. During our initial visit, I kept Fozzie on a very short leash, far enough away so that John trusted that Fozzie would not be able to jump up on him. John was able to relax once we

removed the fear of being jumped on. Eventually, he was able to pet Fozzie. John also became an expert at firmly requesting that people not allow their dogs to jump up on him.

2. Emily, age six, didn't like dogs looking at her. During her sessions, I kept Fozzie facing me, and she was able to observe him from a distance. Slowly, she became more comfortable with being close to Fozzie, and we encouraged her to look at him by asking questions such as "How many different colors make up Fozzie's fur?" and "Is Fozzie's tail curly or straight?" Eventually we asked her "What color are Fozzie's eyes?" She was able to look and say "brown." We praised her and talked about how she was conquering her fear and being very brave.

How You Can Support Your Fearful Child

Validate your child's fear, accept it, and let them know you understand that they are afraid. Do not try to talk them out of it. This will only cause them to try to convince you that they are truly afraid.
Let your child know that you understand that being afraid is not fun. Explain that it is getting in the way of their day-to-day life. Most importantly, let them know that you have confidence in their ability to address the fear and overcome it.

Many children, due to their age or personality, will not have the language skills to express the details of their fears. They may need their parents to "lead the witness." For these kids, parents need to offer observations of their children's fearful behavior or ideas about what they think their children may find scary about dogs. We can help give children an emotional vocabulary to express their concerns, feelings of stress, and level of fear.

It is also helpful for parents to remember a time when they themselves felt afraid, and to share those feelings with their children. With Becky, I used the example of my being afraid to dive off the diving board for the first time. I described the physical sensations of having "butterflies" in my stomach and my heart pounding. I then explained that my mother encouraged me to try it, and how brave and proud I felt afterward.

Fear Scale

In my practice, I ask children to describe their fear on a scale of 1 to 10.

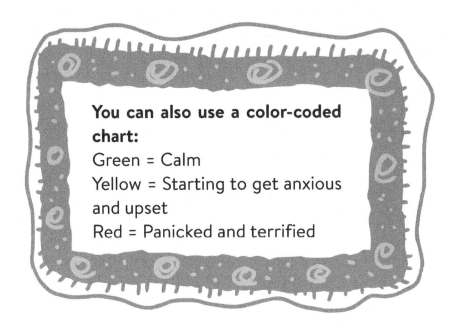

You can also use a color-coded chart:
Green = Calm
Yellow = Starting to get anxious and upset
Red = Panicked and terrified

We need to help children tune in to the physical symptoms of fear and stress. This helps children recognize how they are feeling by listening to what their body is telling them. The physical feelings of fear may include a pounding heart, trouble breathing, nausea, and crying.

Eight-year-old Levi's experience is a good example of a child not being able to express his fear verbally. All Levi could say about dogs was that he didn't like them and that he was scared of them. His fear was so strong that he would scream whenever he saw one. Levi's father filled out the questionnaire to narrow down exactly what Levi's fear encompassed. However, in Levi's case, his fear seemed to apply to all dogs in all situations. We increased his exposure to dogs very slowly. Some children need more time than others to overcome their fear of dogs.

Other children are able to overcome their fears more swiftly. Evan, also age eight, moved quickly through the Overcoming the Fear of Dogs Protocol and received his certificate in one 45-minute session.

Evan's fear was based on his friend telling him about having been bitten by a dog. Evan was highly motivated to overcome his fear because he felt embarrassed by his fear of a dog that was allowed to roam freely at his summer camp. After Evan interacted with Fozzie, who is gentle and well-behaved, he realized that most dogs are safe to be around, including the camp dog.

Through support, encouragement, education, and exposure therapy, most children will learn to be less afraid. For the purposes of this book, my goal is to help children feel less distress around dogs and tolerate being in the proximity of dogs. Some will be happy to interact with dogs and pet them, while other children may feel they need to keep their distance, but are able to be around dogs without experiencing panic.

The next chapter explores the importance of going from fearful to empowered when you help your child face their fear of dogs.

Do's and Don'ts for Parents

- ❑ **Do** educate yourself and your child about dog behaviors and safety around dogs.
- ❑ **Do** accept that your child is afraid of dogs, even if it seems silly or irrational to you.
- ❑ **Do** talk about bravery and explain that being brave means being afraid but doing what you are afraid of anyway.
- ❑ **Do** remember that words have power.
- ❑ **Do** explain that you understand and want to help. Support your child and plant seeds of success by saying things like "I know you are brave, and together we will help you feel more comfortable around dogs."
- ❑ **Do** use positive words and phrases whenever possible, such as "we're working on being more comfortable with dogs" instead of "stop feeling afraid." This is subtle, but it relays an important message.
- ❑ **Do** go at your child's pace.

- ❑ **Do** give your child permission to take a break and speak up when they feel uncomfortable.
- ❑ **Do** establish trust and help your child feel in control. When your child trusts you and feels in control, it helps them to relax and participate in the sessions, which will gradually lessen their fear.
- ❑ **Do** find your child's motivation. Are they motivated to overcome their fear so they can go on a sleepover, visit a relative's house, or be at the school bus stop with a friend's dog?
- ❑ **Do** find a motivational reward your child will work towards. For some, it's the promise of special treats, like ice cream, a new video game, or even money. Not all children require a material reward. For some, praise and increased self-confidence will be enough.
- ❑ **Do** help your child see how dogs are similar to children. This helps children feel empathy toward dogs. Explain that dogs have feelings. They need food, water, exercise, medical care, and — most importantly — love.
- ❑ **Do** help your child see that dogs depend on people to take care of them for their whole lives.
- ❑ **Do** give homework and exercises between formal exposure sessions to help fortify the exposure.
- ❑ **Don't** try to talk your child out of their fear.
- ❑ **Don't** tease or belittle your child.
- ❑ **NEVER** get a dog until your child's fear has decreased enough so that they feel comfortable having a dog. Even then, I strongly recommend "borrowing" a friend's or relative's dog for a few days before considering getting your own dog. This will make sure your child can tolerate being around one for an extended period of time.

Chapter 3:
The Importance Of Overcoming The Fear of Dogs

"You'll never do a whole lot unless you're brave enough to try."
—Dolly Parton

"Thanks to great coaching and support from Stefani, our daughter went from being highly anxious in any room with dogs to brushing, petting, feeding, and even walking Fozzie. It was amazing to see her face her fears and develop new confidence. It also taught her methods for overcoming any other fears that she may have in the future — so this experience has built life skills even beyond comfort with dogs."
—Jeff W. and Jennifer G., Hastings-on-Hudson, NY

Many fears go away as children grow older. They learn to cope with the anxiety and fears that come and go with daily life. Most children eventually learn to do things independently from their parents, such as sleeping in the dark and tolerating thunderstorms.

Children also learn to express their concerns. They learn to accept their parents' assurances that there are no monsters or witches. It is common for children to be wary of putting their heads underwater when they are learning to swim. Once they do, however, learning to swim is usually smooth sailing, and they never think twice about putting their heads underwater again. They may feel nervous before a dance recital but then rally and complete the performance.

Overcoming challenges like these reminds children that the next time they have a big event or an assignment that feels intimidating, they were able to perform in the dance recital and swim underwater, so they can rise to this challenge also. This builds resilience.

But often when a child has a strong fear of dogs, they don't grow out of it. It requires some form of intervention. When children are afraid of dogs, they try to avoid them at all costs. By not exposing children to friendly and safe dogs, many well-intentioned parents inadvertently reinforce the fear. This, as you will see, is the direct opposite of what they should be doing to help their child. If left untreated, the fear of dogs can turn into a significant source of anxiety, family discord, and social stress.

As previously discussed, it is virtually impossible to avoid all contact with dogs. However, many kids who are afraid of dogs will try very hard to do so. While dogs are the actual trigger for the fear, these children spend a lot of emotional energy worrying about running into a dog or planning excuses to use if they have to go somewhere where there might be dogs.

If the fear is not addressed, a phobia can develop, which can have a significant impact on not only the child's daily life but also on their future. For example, I worked with an 18-year-old young man who was doing a college internship at a start-up tech company. The owners of the company brought their dogs to the office with them. The young man considered quitting the position because his fear was so strong. Not only was he afraid of the dogs themselves, he felt ashamed and embarrassed by his strong fear reaction to the dogs. We worked together for a short time, and he went on to get his degree — he now works for the same company full time!

The Cost of Being Afraid
Constant Stress: Fight-or-Flight

Walking around with fear takes a terrible toll on children and affects all aspects of their lives: physical, emotional, and social.

The fight-or-flight response has been part of our biology since early human history. It is a neurological response that was helpful during prehistoric times when a person encountered a dangerous situation, such as a bear or an armed warrior. An instantaneous decision had to be made to stay and **fight** or run away and flee **(flight)**. The body prepares for this fight-or-flight response by raising the heart rate to pump blood to the arms and legs and flooding the body with adrenaline to give us more energy and strength.

Children who are phobic of dogs often go into the panic mode of fight-or-flight. This experience is physically exhausting and emotionally draining. Talking the child through the experience with relaxation exercises, such as taking deep breaths, can help calm this neurological reaction. However, if the fear continues and develops into a constant worry, the body stays in a perpetual state of stress in the fight-or-flight mode.

When children feel anxious, they are often continuously worried about the possibility of something bad happening to them or coming into contact with their feared object. They can become hypervigilant about their environment and extremely observant of everything around them. This can interfere with their daily lives and prevent them from enjoying themselves. It is exhausting to walk around in a heightened state of fear, constantly worried that a dog might get loose at the park, that they will be invited to a sleepover where there are dogs, or that their friends might tease them about their fear.

According to the U.S. National Library of Medicine, signs of a heightened state of stress include — but are not limited to — these physical symptoms: [3]

- ❑ Decreased appetite or other changes in eating habits
- ❑ Headaches
- ❑ New or recurrent bed-wetting
- ❑ Sleep disturbances or nightmares
- ❑ Upset stomach or vague stomach pain

Emotional or behavioral symptoms may include:

- ❑ Anxiety, worry
- ❑ Inability to relax
- ❑ New or recurring fears (in this case, fear of dogs)
- ❑ Clinging, unwillingness to let parents/guardians out of sight
- ❑ Anger, crying, whining
- ❑ Inability to control emotions
- ❑ Aggressive or stubborn behavior
- ❑ Going back to behaviors from a younger age
- ❑ Refusal to participate in family or school activities

In some cases, children want to keep their fears a secret because they are embarrassed or ashamed. Sometimes they try to hide their fears because they are worried that well-meaning adults will force them into stressful situations.

Note to parents:

Resist the urge to force your child to face their fear of dogs without consulting the questionnaire in this book and/or professional advice first. You don't want your good intentions to go awry and increase your child's fear and stress. This is a process that takes time and patience.

The Shame Factor

According to Kenneth Barish, Ph.D., an expert on child psychology, "Shame is our instinctive response to personal failure or inadequacy, especially the public exposure of inadequacy. Embarrassment is a temporary and mild form of shame; humiliation, aloneness, and self-hatred are severe forms of shame. In childhood, shame leads to avoidance and withdrawal.... Many experiences that evoke a feeling of shame (for example, experiences of exclusion or ridicule) are uniquely painful, and the feeling of shame, perhaps more than any other emotion, stays with us."[4]

Being afraid of dogs often leads to feelings of shame when children see that most people enjoy dogs. The child then wonders what is wrong with them. Most people do not fully understand the debilitating level of fear these children feel, and they may discount it or minimize it. Unfortunately, these children may be teased or bullied.

For example, our family friends had a lovely pug, and whenever we were invited to their home, the mother inadvertently made my daughter Becky feel ashamed of her fear of dogs. She would say things like "Why are you so afraid? Barney is so cute and friendly, just pet him, you'll see." It was important for Becky's father and myself to support Becky and ensure that her self-esteem wasn't damaged. We came up with some rehearsed lines that would help empower Becky. We would say, "Becky is a sensitive kid, and we are taking it slow and helping her learn about being near dogs."

The flip side of shame is pride, which is a highly desirable emotion and helps guarantee healthy self-esteem. I see this a lot when kids are finally able to pet Fozzie. They beam with pride. I also saw it when Becky was finally able to say she wasn't afraid of dogs anymore!

Benefits of Overcoming Fear

There is much to gain when children overcome their fears. They gain self-confidence and self-esteem. They learn to cope with their fears and anxieties. Coping skills and having self-control are two of the biggest predictors of success later in life, according to a study by Duke University psychologist Terrie Moffit.[5]

In my thirty years of working with children, I have observed that children who conquer fear:

- ❑ Learn to speak up and ask for help
- ❑ Become aware of their feelings and express them accurately
- ❑ Turn to relaxation techniques to help them deal with uncomfortable feelings
- ❑ Develop trust
- ❑ Strengthen their relationships with their parents, family, and friends
- ❑ Learn to be true to themselves and their feelings

During my therapy sessions with children, working with or without dogs, I teach coping strategies. These coping strategies help children achieve a sense of calm and control, especially when faced with a stressful situation. They can continue to use these coping strategies throughout their lives.

Mindfulness has become a buzzword in the last few years and is practiced in homes and classrooms all over the world. When we are mindful, we are totally focused on the present in a non-judgmental and loving way. Mindfulness exercises help us regulate our emotions and our bodies. For kids who are experiencing distress and fear, mindfulness techniques and exercises can help them calm down and bring them back to the present. There are many exercises to help children (and adults) accomplish this. Here are a few that I use routinely in my social work practice.

Mindfulness and Relaxation Exercises to Help Your Child Decrease Stress and Anxiety Levels

Technique #1

Focusing on Breathing

Take deep belly breaths. Focus on the in-and-out motion of your breathing. This helps you focus your attention and calm your body. Breathe in for a count of four and out for a count of four. When working with young children, I often tell them to "smell the flowers" to get them to take a deep breath in through their nose and then "blow out the birthday candles" to describe a big exhale.

Another one that kids like is known as "hand breathing." Using their non-dominant hand, have the child spread their fingers out wide. Next, have them use their dominant hand's index finger to slowly trace up and down each finger on the other hand. Each time they move their finger up they breathe in and when they move it down they breathe out.

Technique #2

Using Your Senses

Find at least two things to experience with your senses. Look around your environment and notice two things you can see, hear, touch, or smell. For example, your child might see a picture on the wall and their parent's hat; hear a bird singing and the hum of the refrigerator, etc. Focusing on their environment for a few minutes allows your child to take a break from their anxiety and other uncomfortable feelings.

Technique #3

Self-talk

Self-talk can be helpful; find a phrase that helps your child feel in control and less anxious. For children, I often recommend "I can handle this!" "No biggie," and "I am okay." When a dog is included in the therapy, you can cue the child to say "Fozzie is a sweet dog, and he likes me."

Technique #4

Imagining You Are at a Favorite Place

Another exercise I use with children who are experiencing any kind of anxiety is to practice going to their "happy place." For this exercise, you tell the child to close their eyes and imagine that they are at a beach, park, camp, or wherever they feel happy. Please be mindful, however, that this is not a practical exercise to do with fearful children if there is a dog nearby, as closing their eyes will only make them feel more vulnerable.

Technique #5

Visualization

Have your child practice visualizing seeing and/or interacting with a dog. This should be done separately from a dog-exposure session. Have your child find a photograph of a dog that they think they might like to pet one day. Encourage your child to close their eyes and relax by taking deep breaths. You can describe a scenario to your child in which this friendly dog is sitting quietly on a leash with its handler. Have your child imagine that they are observing the dog and gradually walking closer and closer, then eventually reaching out to touch the dog.

Providing children with tools and techniques to help themselves is very important. When children feel that they are capable and competent, they tend to have higher self-esteem and are more willing to try new things. They are also more resilient, which means they bounce back more quickly when things don't go their way. There are many opportunities available for children to practice resilience, such as sports, gaming, chess, and the arts. It takes a lot of confidence to try out for the orchestra or the lacrosse team, and courage to not give up when they don't succeed right away.

Parents should help their children feel competent and independent. One easy way to encourage independence is to give your child two appropriate choices. Toddlers, for example, can choose what kind of cereal they want. Preschoolers can pick out a shirt or a snack they want. Grade-schoolers can pick an after-school club. The important word here is "appropriate." Please don't ask your child if they want to wear dressy pants *or* tracksuit pants if the only acceptable answer is tracksuit pants. Allow them to choose between two options that are equally okay.

When you give your child options, you are letting them know that you have confidence in their ability to make a good choice. You can ask an older child their opinion on what to get Grandma for her birthday, for example. This demonstrates your interest and confidence in what your child has to say. **Every day of being a parent affords many opportunities to help or hinder your child's self-esteem, confidence, and competence.** In addition to feeling that they can do age-appropriate things for themselves, children need to understand their feelings.

A child's ability to manage their feelings and their behavior is called self-regulation. Part of growing up is learning how to master strong feelings, to sit through a classroom lesson, to raise our hand instead of calling out, and to share the ball during a pick-up basketball game. Children who can handle disappointment, delay gratification, and wait their turn have a leg up on the children who are impulsive and emotionally reactive. Self-regulation comes more easily to some kids than others, but all kids can benefit from having parents and teachers who model these skills and help children develop them.

I have seen many parents who are quick to try to fix things for their children because they want to prevent their child from getting upset. The "everyone gets a trophy" mindset developed out of this mentality because parents wanted to protect their child's feelings. While this is a noble idea, it actually cheats children out of learning to cope with strong feelings. Many *adults* have never learned to handle difficult and strong emotions such as disappointment, anger, and loss. Children can learn to handle these difficult feelings with the support of their parents, but in order to practice these coping skills, children need to experience the intense feelings. When parents swoop in to rescue children or "fix" situations that may upset them, their child receives the message that they are unable to handle the situation, and this lowers their self-confidence. Childhood provides the opportunity for children to learn how to handle uncomfortable feelings and challenging situations in small steps with parents as a safety net in case they fall.

From Fearful to Empowered

When kids overcome their fears, they feel brave, empowered, and confident. Remember that being brave is not the same as not being afraid. Rather, it is feeling afraid and being able to do the scary thing anyway. Not all children who overcome their fears will want to run out and get a dog, but their general stress and anxiety levels should decrease. They will no longer have to worry about dogs at the bus stop or Farmers Market. Feeling empowered, they can readily accept invitations to homes that have dogs or go to the park with friends. Emotional energy will be freed up because they are no longer funneling that energy into worrying about encountering dogs.

Through thoughtful exposure therapy, children begin to see that they **are** safe around dogs and they can begin to let their guard down.

Children who are able to eventually interact with dogs gain even more. Dogs offer their human families unconditional love, and studies have shown that petting a dog can reduce stress and lower blood pressure. According to the Pet Health Council[6], "Kids who have pets have higher self-esteem and improved social skills. Children with low self-esteem may talk to or confide in an animal in ways they would not with people. They are often more confident in performing tasks they find difficult with an animal simply because the animal does not care if mistakes are made, nor will the child be afraid of looking silly in front of the animal." This is the premise behind programs in which children read to dogs. (Chapter Eight will discuss additional benefits of the human-animal relationship and bond.)

In Chapter Five, I use Ryan's story as a case study to illustrate the OFOD Protocol. His story is a perfect example of a child who struggled with fear but was able to eventually overcome it. He felt immense pride as a result. Ryan rated himself at a 10 on the Fear Scale when he first saw Fozzie. I kept Fozzie in a lying-down "stay" position for most of the session. Ryan practiced breathing exercises, and we chatted about things not directly related to dogs for about half of the session. I asked Ryan to do some deep breathing and look around the room and state two things he saw, heard, touched, and smelled. Immediately, Ryan's fear and anxiety levels came down a bit.

Eventually, Ryan was able to sit on his father's lap and reach out and touch Fozzie's rump with one finger. Ryan expressed that he did not want the dog to look at him, so I kept Fozzie focused on me. Ryan's sense of relief was visible on his face, and his wide smile showed how proud he felt. It was important to have Ryan touch Fozzie a few more times to decrease his resistance and increase his confidence. Ryan said his level of fear had come down to about a 4 at the end of the session. You can read Ryan's full case study in the protocol section of this book.

Some children may experience an improvement with their fear of dogs quickly. For others, it may take several sessions. Every child is different and needs to proceed in their own time.

In the next chapter of this book, we will look at how to determine the best methods and strategies for helping your child overcome their fear of dogs. It all begins with understanding your role as a parent and what you should and shouldn't do in order to help your child go through this important process.

Chapter 4:
Addressing Your Child's Fear Of Dogs

"Nothing in life is to be feared. It is only to be understood."

—Marie Curie

"I was really afraid to work with Stefani and Fozzie and even felt sick to my stomach about it. But I am really glad I did it because my whole life changed."

—Ryan, age 8

This chapter will help prepare you for implementing my protocol for Overcoming the Fear of Dogs (OFOD). By exploring strategies such as goal-setting, positive reinforcement, and recognizing your child's readiness, this guide will help ensure that the exposure therapy is successful. We will explore your role in the techniques as well as the role of the dog and his or her handler.

There will most likely be four individuals involved in your child's therapy exercises:

1. Your child.
2. A well-trained dog with a calm temperament suited to the exercises.
3. A dog handler who understands the needs of the dog and knows how to manage the dog well.
4. You or another adult who is willing and able to help your child overcome their fear of dogs.

One option is to work with a therapist, a well-trained therapy dog, and the dog's handler for a session or two. In this way, you can help your child stay calm and feel supported. A good therapist for this role should be trained in anxiety and exposure therapy and is comfortable working with children. Therapists are trained and, therefore, should be able to stay emotionally neutral as they help guide and facilitate the session. A therapist can also provide helpful observations about your child and the process in an objective manner. To find a therapist and/or a therapy dog and handler, please see the list of resources at the back of this book.

YOUR ROLE
Understanding Your Role

Helping your child overcome their fear of dogs may be an opportunity to strengthen the bond between you and your child. Your role involves learning how best to support your child and to help them work through fears and manage difficult feelings. Together, you will also learn a lot about dogs. A client recently reminded me of something I said when we began working together. I had pointed out that her child (who has a debilitating genetic disorder) will have many therapists and teachers throughout her life, but she will only have one mother.

In order to accomplish the goal of helping your child overcome their fear of dogs, your role will be to act as your child's helper. You will facilitate interactions between your child and the dog. Eventually, these interactions may include more than one dog or visits to places in your community where many people bring their dogs, such as the park or the Farmers Market.

If you haven't already, now would be a good time to take a close look at how **you** feel about dogs and being near them. If you are 100% comfortable around most dogs and can go at your child's pace, then you can designate yourself as the helper adult. If you are easily frustrated, or if you and your child get into frequent power struggles or other arguments (all of which are perfectly normal), it would be best to find another adult to act as your child's helper. Decide on your role and try to stick to it unless you find the sessions aren't going well (in this case you can find another adult to help). I have found that the parents best suited for this activity are those who can advocate for their children but also allow them to express their needs.

The story of Rosie and her family is a good example of how important it is to find the right human and canine helpers. Rosie's father called me from a neighboring state to talk about his seven-year-old daughter Rosie's fear of dogs.

Rosie's Story, Age Seven

Rosie's dad, Mr. Rothman, had grown up with dogs and hoped to have one join their family. He described Rosie as a happy and confident child — unless she came into contact with a dog. The Rothmans lived too far away for me to work with them in person. Through email and phone conversations, I was able to provide them with exposure exercises and guidelines. I encouraged Mr. Rothman to do a thorough assessment of Rosie's fear and to find a suitable helper dog for the exercises.

Mr. Rothman mentioned that his mother had a gentle older poodle mix that was usually crated when the family visited because Rosie was so fearful. I spoke with Mr. Rothman's mother, Barbara, and was confident that her dog, Moxie, would be suitable for the therapy exercises. In addition, I felt Mrs. Rothman would be able to balance her love of her dog with the needs of her granddaughter by being patient with Rosie and not pushing Moxie on her. I outlined the exercises in the OFOD Protocol and laid out some ground rules:

Always keep Moxie on a leash and let Rosie decide how close she wants to get to the dog. I also identified ways to reinforce Rosie's success by increasing the length and intensity of exposure. It took several weeks of supervised interactions with Moxie while the dog was leashed, but eventually, Rosie felt comfortable enough to be in her grandmother's apartment with Moxie roaming freely. The family agreed that whenever Rosie felt too nervous about the dog, all she had to do was ask that Moxie be leashed or crated. According to Mr. Rothman, Rosie only felt the need to ask this on one occasion.

Mr. Rothman later emailed to say that the family had worked with a dog trainer to find the perfect dog for them. They adopted a medium-sized, mixed-breed dog who was being fostered because his original family was moving.

Finding a dog that is being cared for in a foster home can be a good way to adopt a dog. The dog avoids the stress and potential trauma of being in a shelter, and the foster family is able to give the prospective adopter a complete picture of the dog's temperament. In this case, the foster family had two children (ages nine and eleven) and a cat. Both the foster family and the Rothmans were fairly confident that the dog would get along well with Rosie (who was nine by this time) and her eleven-year-old brother. The Rothmans named the dog Mason, and now he sleeps on Rosie's bed!

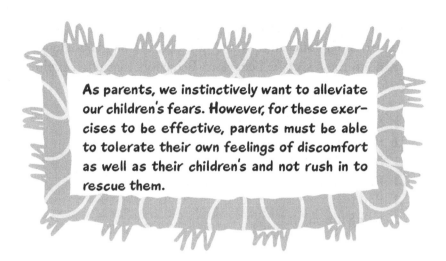

As parents, we instinctively want to alleviate our children's fears. However, for these exercises to be effective, parents must be able to tolerate their own feelings of discomfort as well as their children's and not rush in to rescue them.

As the helper, you need to balance your child's behaviors and emotions as well as your own behaviors and thoughts. If you are working with a dog you know, you must be able to "read" the dog's emotions and intentions through his behavior and manage his activity. It is a lot, even for me, to balance all of this during exposure sessions. For this reason, I highly recommend finding someone with a well-behaved dog who can support you and your child through this process.

The adult helper should visualize putting on a coach's hat, then take a deep breath and be ready to model healthy interactions with a dog, encouraging and gently nudging your child out of their comfort zone as the therapy team moves through the exposure exercises together. If you feel you aren't the best person for the job, find a relative, friend, therapist, or dog trainer who can work through the steps in this book with your child and the helper dog.

Remember to be safe and exercise appropriate caution whenever you are interacting with dogs or any live animals.

When selecting a dog to work with, keep in mind the specific behaviors that frighten your child. Make sure that the dog you choose is not prone to these specific behaviors. Behaviors that often frighten children include:

- [ ] Being licked
- [ ] Being jumped up on
- [ ] Being chased
- [ ] Being bitten
- [ ] Barking
- [ ] Being lunged at

> Always thank your child for telling you what they are experiencing. In addition to making your child feel heard and validated, this technique helps you understand how to proceed. At the same time, it helps to build trust.

Structure and predictability are important

When working with a dog, always let your child know what you are going to do *before* you do it. This will help reduce your child's anxiety and allow them to participate fully in the process. In order for your child to trust the process and to let their guard down, they need to trust that there will be no surprises. Outline the goals and activities of the exposure ahead of time. During the session, talk about how things are proceeding and what they can expect next as the session progresses. Remember, anxiety comes from feeling that you are not in control. Help your child have appropriate control of the sessions by informing them of what is happening and what will happen next.

You may be wondering how you will know if you are doing the exercises correctly. You will know by your child's demeanor and their willingness to continue participating in the exercises.

Have the right mindset; speak in positive words

Our attitudes and beliefs about what we can and can't do really make a difference. When we reframe our words, we reframe our thoughts. In her book, *Mindset*, Dr. Carol Dweck explores the importance of having a "growth mindset." She defines this as "the belief that your basic qualities are things you can cultivate through your efforts, your strategies and help from others."[7]

One of the things we can do to empower children to overcome their fear of dogs is to help them believe that they **can** do it. You need to believe it as well. When your child says, "I can't be near dogs, they scare me too much," encourage them to start changing that statement to "this may take some time and effort, but I can do it." Or, "I'm learning to feel safe and comfortable around dogs." Having a growth mindset is important for kids to gain confidence so they don't get discouraged and give up. Believing they will ultimately be able to go on a sleepover or walk past a leashed dog will help your child stick with the process. Having confidence in one's ability to handle challenges is a very important life skill. When my daughter Becky felt anxious about trying new things or going to new places, we often prompted her to "remember when you were afraid of dogs, and you were so brave and pushed through it? You can do the same thing here."

Have your child say daily affirmations, such as "I am brave," and "I like dogs, and dogs like me."

Checklist for Parent/Helper Before Each Session:

1. **Center yourself. Be prepared and present.**

2. **Remind yourself to be patient and to use encouragement, not pressure.**

3. **Express to the child that you, the dog, and the dog's handler are all on the child's team.**

4. **Remind the child that dogs are more similar to children than they think.**

5. **Have a specific goal in mind, like petting the dog with a full hand or brushing him.**

6. **Be prepared to think and proceed in baby steps.**
   Every interaction — even moving six inches closer to the dog or looking at the dog — *is progress.*

7. **Learn how to read dog body language.**

8. **Be prepared to demonstrate appropriate ways to interact with the dog.**
   Remember to be calm around dogs and aware of their body language and behavior.

9. **Always model effective coping skills including relaxation techniques.**
   Children are mirrors; they learn a lot about the world from watching us. Model deep breathing, saying affirmations out loud (such as "I can do this"), and narrating your progress.

10. **Keep a log of exercises and describe the progress you make in each session.**
    You can use the form provided in the Resource Section to keep track of your progress.

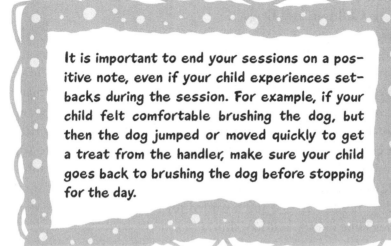

It is important to end your sessions on a positive note, even if your child experiences setbacks during the session. For example, if your child felt comfortable brushing the dog, but then the dog jumped or moved quickly to get a treat from the handler, make sure your child goes back to brushing the dog before stopping for the day.

As noted above, your child needs to feel that they have control during the session. That's why it's important to include your child's input in planning the session: let them decide how close they want to be to the dog when the session starts and ask what they hope to accomplish by the end of the session.

You will need to strike a balance between giving your child control over their interactions with the dog and gently nudging them to try something that's out of their comfort zone, where they will feel a little out of control.

When you first begin to address your child's fear, be prepared for a lot of push-back, resistance, and flat-out refusals to interact with the dog. This is the fear talking. By going slowly and using the guidelines to work through the process, your child should be able to make some progress each session.

Exercise: Lunchbox to Demonstrate Similarities between Children and Dogs

For this exercise, I fill a small bag or lunchbox with both real and toy versions of items that dogs need. The overall purpose of the lunchbox exercise is to show the child that dogs and kids need and like many of the same things. I include two doll-sized bowls (one for water and one for food); a soft brush designed for babies (the softness of the brush ensures that if the child brushes the dog, the experience will be comfortable for the dog); a leash, collar, and ID tag; a toy stethoscope (to show that dogs go to the doctor, too); a toy bone (to show that dogs need to chew); and a stuffed toy or ball (to show children that dogs like to play and have fun).

When working with Fozzie, I use a stuffed animal toy rather than a ball because Fozzie gets very excited when playing with balls and can't always be trusted to play gently with them. This is an example of why it's essential to know the dog you are working with, to prevent any possible hiccups.

Things to Keep in Mind When Working with Your Child

- ❑ Accept your child's fears and concerns.
- ❑ Believe in your child's ability to overcome their fear.
- ❑ Don't label your child as fearful.
- ❑ Use positive language such as "we are working on liking dogs better" or "you are learning to be more comfortable around dogs." The words you choose have a strong impact. If your child keeps hearing that they are afraid of dogs, they will believe it even more strongly.
- ❑ Don't talk about your child's fear in front of them unless you are including them in a supportive conversation.
- ❑ Go at your child's pace, not yours.

As Mary Kay Ash, the founder of Mary Kay Cosmetics, said, "If you think you can, you can. If you think you can't, you're right."[8]

Help your child recite "I can do this" over and over again — and eventually they will!

Isabela's Story, Age Ten

Isabela's story shows the importance of moving at your child's pace and demonstrating confidence in their ability to overcome their fear. Isabela's mother, Janet, described her own anxiety about helping her daughter overcome her fear of dogs. "I was so nervous to get started with you and Fozzie. I worried that Isabela would just cry and scream and refuse to touch Fozzie. He is so sweet, and you were so patient. I finally realized that if we went very slowly and encouraged her at every turn, she would eventually touch the dog. Then, what I couldn't believe, is once Isabela touched Fozzie, she went through the exercises pretty quickly. I am so glad we didn't force her to touch him, and also that we no longer have to avoid dogs!"

SET GOALS

Each exposure therapy session should be structured around a specific goal.

Exposure therapy is a process of increased exposure and interactions with dogs. When one goal is achieved, you set another and then another until your child is comfortable around dogs.

Here are three goals that you can use at the beginning of your child's desensitization process. They are part of the OFOD Protocol found in Chapter Five.

GOAL #1
Be in close proximity to the dog.

This is the goal of the first session. In order to use exposure therapy with a live dog, the child must be near the dog. Some kids will need to start from farther away than others in order to feel safe while looking at the dog. In some extreme cases, I keep Fozzie in my car (weather permitting and with the window partially down), and have the child view him from outside the car. This allows the child to reduce the fear of being near a dog because there is a barrier. The majority of our sessions start out with Fozzie and I standing about six to ten feet away from the child. During the 45-minute session, we gradually close the gap, depending on the child's comfort level.

GOAL #2
Have your child give a verbal command like "sit" or "down."

When a child gives a dog a command and then watches the dog obey, it gives the child a sense of control and pride. The handler may need to give a subtle hand signal to the dog to ensure that the dog obeys the child's verbal cue. Knowing that they can ask the dog to sit or lie down at any point in the session will help the child feel more secure. This can be used as a safety valve throughout the therapy process. Whenever something feels too scary or threatening, the child can always ask the dog to sit.

Seven-year-old Aiesha used this technique to manage her anxiety. After she had successfully completed the goals of being near a stationary dog, then petting and brushing him, we moved on to having her be near Fozzie while I walked him around the room on a leash. When Aiesha felt that the dog was getting too close, she would ask him to sit. She learned to say his name first to get his attention, then give him the command: "Fozzie — sit!"

GOAL #3
Brushing the dog.

For this exercise, you will need two brushes with soft bristles. I use brushes made for babies' hair. They usually have cute pictures on them — one of my brushes has Winnie the Pooh on it and the other has Elmo. Asking the child to choose a brush gives them a quick break from feeling anxious. Give the child the option of brushing the dog in two different areas of the body. Check with the handler to make sure you choose areas that the dog likes having brushed. Some children will feel comfortable brushing the dog right away, while others will need to work up to it. As with all interactions, it is helpful to break down the goal into manageable pieces.

One way to approach this exercise is to have the child hold your wrist while you brush the dog, so that you brush the dog together. Gradually increase the number of brush strokes. Then have the child hold the brush while you hold the child's wrist until the child is comfortable brushing on their own.

Tools You Can Use to Help Facilitate the Child's Interactions with the Dog

Tool #1
Engage your child's curiosity.

Ask the child questions, such as "why do you think the dog is sniffing around my feet?" or "how do you think Fozzie is feeling right now?" When a child engages the thinking part of their brain, it gives the anxious part a break. They are able to focus on what is happening in the moment and are less worried about what might happen.

Tool #2
Use encouragement, mantras, and affirmations.

Examples of encouraging statements are: "I know this is hard, but you can do it. You mastered tricky and scary things before!"

Mantras are short statements children can repeat to themselves during the process, such as "I will try," "I can handle it," and "I'm doing it!"

Affirmations are positive statements that help build confidence in the process. I often have children use the affirmation "I am a brave kid and I like dogs!"

Tool #3
Have a growth mindset.

Instead of…	Try thinking…
This is too scary.	This may take some time and effort.
I give up.	I'm going to train my brain to be brave.
This won't work.	I accept this challenge.

Tool #4
Have rehearsed responses ready for any questions your child may have.

If your child asks if the dog will jump on them, you can say something like "the dog will be on a leash the whole time, and I will make sure he doesn't jump on you." It's also helpful to be able to explain why dogs behave the way they do, especially when you know the particular dog is prone to a specific behavior that may be a bit challenging for the child. For example, my dog Fozzie occasionally does a little jump near me to get my attention. This might happen if he thinks the treats aren't coming fast enough. When this happens, I explain to the child that he sometimes has difficulty waiting for treats. Once they understand why Fozzie jumped, they become less afraid. I also help them understand by explaining that it's often hard for a child to have to wait patiently for a cookie, too.

Having a reliable and practiced response ready will help your child relax and trust the process. You will also be more relaxed if you know what to say and won't worry about being caught off-guard. Your child will sense you're at ease, and that will help them feel more relaxed as well.

These are common questions that you may be asked. I have included how I typically answer with regards to Fozzie. You can use these as a starting point and modify your responses based on the helper dog and the situation.

1. **Does the dog bite?**
    All dogs can bite, so we need to be respectful and careful around them. I can assure you that Fozzie will not bite. He has been temperament-tested and is very patient.

    It is vital that the helper dog does not have a history of biting. Please make sure that the child is respectful of the dog and does not pull the dog's tail or tease the dog, for example.

2. **Will the dog lick me?**

Fozzie doesn't lick unless you have cream cheese or something similarly delicious on your fingers or face. So, I can say for sure that he will not.

Some dogs are lickers. In this case, you can say "I will watch him closely and try to make sure the dog doesn't lick you." You should know beforehand if licking is one of the child's specific fears. If so, choose an appropriate dog that isn't inclined to lick.

3. **Will the dog jump on me?**

Fozzie will not jump on you because he will be on a leash the whole time. I will make sure he doesn't jump on you. I also watch his behavior, so if it looks like he is getting excited and you start to feel scared, I can give him a break outside.

Please be sure to choose a helper dog that doesn't jump on people or lunge while on a leash.

4. **Will the dog bark?**

Fozzie barks because he has something to say. This is one way dogs communicate. Dogs bark for many reasons. Some dogs bark to let you know that someone is at the door or a package is being delivered. Some dogs bark when they see a friend — either human or another dog. If Fozzie barks, I will help you understand what he is saying. We can be detectives and figure out what he wants to tell us.

Find out from the handler if the helper dog is likely to bark and under what circumstances so that you can be prepared to explain it to your child.

5. **Is the dog dangerous?**

   This is an excellent question. I am 100% positive that Fozzie is not dangerous. In fact, he loves kids and enjoys his work helping you feel comfortable near dogs.

   If you are not able to give a resounding "No, he is safe to be around," then the dog should not go anywhere near your child or any other child. You can thank your child for asking the question, then reassure your child that you would not bring a dangerous dog anywhere near them, and in fact, *you* would not want to be near a dangerous dog, either. In addition, let your child know that you are going to make sure that everyone involved in the session, including the dog, will be safe.

Tool #5
Provide education and information on dog body language and behavior.

> Important: Kids need information so that they can understand the dog's behavior and the situation.
>
> Remember: We are less afraid of things we understand.

Post-Session Debriefing

It's important to take some time after the session to explore and discuss with your child their experiences during the session. Praise your child again for the progress they made. Ask how they thought it went. Remember to reinforce their *effort* as well, especially if they made limited progress.

Tell your child, "I could see you were really trying." Ask your child to use the Fear Scale to describe their level of fear at the beginning and at the end of the session. Ask if there were times during the session where the fear level fluctuated. You will most likely find that at the beginning of the next session the fear level will be up again, but hopefully not as high as it was the first time. It should come down more quickly during subsequent sessions.

Review which exercises and strategies are helping. What made your child feel proud? Are there some activities that caused too much stress? This type of debriefing will give you important guidance and information on how to proceed with the next stages of the process. Please refer to the *Session Log* in the Resource Section to document the session and plan for the next one.

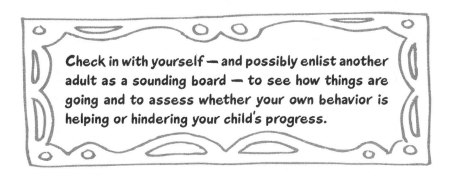

Check in with yourself — and possibly enlist another adult as a sounding board — to see how things are going and to assess whether your own behavior is helping or hindering your child's progress.

It's key to filter the advice of others.

Other people may want to offer advice, but they are not as aware as you are of the process. You know your child best and you know their pace. Resist pressure from others and honor your child's needs. Your Aunt Barbara might suggest going to the dog park, which sounds like a good idea to her, but could be far too scary for a fearful child. Some well-meaning dog owners may encourage their dogs to get close to your child to prove their dog is nice, but this may overwhelm your child and increase their fear.

Even family doctors don't always know the best way to handle children's fears. One pediatrician I know told a family who had a child that was afraid of dogs to "just get a dog." The parents followed the doctor's advice and it ended up amplifying their child's fear and causing the child to distrust her parents and the doctor.

Be patient and stay the course. It is okay to tell these well-meaning people that you appreciate their desire to help, but you are following a specific OFOD Protocol based on exposure therapy that was developed by an expert in this area. (Then show them this book!)

Helpful Tips for a Successful Session

- ☐ Stay calm.
- ☐ Tune in to your child's fear level.
- ☐ Follow the protocol.
- ☐ Check in with your child frequently during the session.
- ☐ Encourage, praise, and reward.
- ☐ Always do whatever is needed to make your child feel comfortable and supported while gently encouraging them to take the next step.
- ☐ Be patient.

If something happens during the session that increases your child's fear, it's important to stay calm and recognize that this is just a natural part of working with dogs (and people!). If a dog jumps up for a treat instead of remaining in a sitting position or the dog looks at your child when this has been discussed as too fearful for your child, take a break and calmly explain to the child why the dog behaved that way.

Explaining the dog's behavior and motivations will help your child better understand what the dog is trying to communicate. The dog may have moved suddenly or looked at your child, but that wasn't because he was going to bite. Explain that the dog moved because he wanted the treat, or that he turned to look at them because he was curious about the kind and gentle child who was brushing him.

Whenever possible, find ways to compare the dog's behavior and motivation to your child's own motivations and behaviors. This will help them understand and relate to the dog, which will help ease their fear. Most kids can relate to the idea that sometimes dogs are like kids who might run up to someone who has a treat for them.

As 12-year-old Kevin put it, "It helped me to be less scared when I understood why Fozzie would wiggle around, even when he was in sitting position. I realized he has ants in his pants, kind of like me!"

Mindfulness and Grounding Exercises

Utilize exercises that help your child stay grounded in the moment when they feel afraid. A child who is willing to face the object of their fear is under a lot of pressure. The Fear Scale will help them express how afraid they feel at any given moment. When your child feels overwhelmed, it may be helpful to take a break from working with the dog. Ask your child to look around and engage their senses. Ask them to find things they can see, hear, touch (this can be the dog, but it doesn't have to be), and smell. Depending on their age, asking children what they smell might be opening up the situation to fart jokes, dog butt giggles, and the like, but this may serve as a tension breaker, so use your judgment. This type of technique is a useful tool for anyone experiencing strong emotions. I practice noticing things with my senses, and I help my clients learn to do this. (More exercises are listed in Chapter Three.)

THE ROLE OF THE DOG HANDLER
Understanding the Role of the Dog Handler

Keep in mind that these exposure exercises will be stressful for your child — and likely for you, as well. Therefore, the dog handler must have certain skills and traits that will allow them to help you with this process.

An ideal dog handler will be patient, have an open mind, and have a willingness to help. They also need to be willing to learn a little bit about cynophobia and anxiety in general and let you (or the therapist if one is involved) lead the exercises.

The handler should have a calm demeanor, be able to keep a constant close eye on the dog, and be able to follow your lead. They should know the dog well and be able to anticipate any "hiccups" in the session. The handler must have excellent control of the dog at all times. They should be understanding and able to think and respond quickly and tactfully to changing situations.

For example, sometimes Fozzie will turn his backside to the child and myself as a way to give himself a break from the session. Instead of saying that Fozzie is tired, bored, or needs something new to sniff, I make light of the situation and say "Oh, look! Fozzie wants a butt scratch."

It is also essential that the handler not take it personally if a child makes criticizing comments about the dog out of fear or resistance to the process. For example, children have said that Fozzie looks old because he has grey fur or that he looks "mean." Remember that kids cannot be talked out of their fear; they need to experience positive interactions to learn for themselves that they can be safe and okay around dogs.

The handler should consider the dog's needs as well. If they see that the dog is tired or stressed, they need to feel comfortable letting you know it's time to give the dog a break. It may be necessary to reschedule the session if the dog is not feeling up to working. Sessions should not be scheduled on days when the dog goes to the groomer or vet. Most therapy dog organizations have guidelines and suggestions for maximizing therapy dog visits. You can find these organizations listed in the Resource Section.

Just like people, dogs can feel tired or stressed. Fozzie's predecessor Mugsy was also a Keeshond and therapy dog. Mugsy and I worked with recreational therapists at a local children's rehabilitation hospital helping children who were recovering from strokes. These children were often passive and sometimes sad, but they perked up whenever they saw Mugsy arrive. Mugsy worked hard at engaging with them, doing tricks, and allowing them to brush him as a way of exercising their arms and hands.

Mugsy loved the work, but it took a lot of energy. Halfway through the sessions, I would say that Mugsy needed water and we would go outside for a quick bathroom break. Mugsy always defecated during these outdoor breaks — which was unusual for him, as he was normally a once-a-day pooper. However, it was a way for him to destress and reset his energy. A less-observant dog handler might not have put two and two together and afforded him this break.

The handler needs to be willing to make a firm commitment to completing the sessions with you and your child, and they should participate in debriefing and planning for future sessions. If you use a professional dog trainer/handler and their dog, you will most likely have to pay for the sessions. If a neighbor, friend, or relative is the helping handler, you can offer them money for their assistance, too. If they prefer not to be paid for their help, they might appreciate a different gesture of thanks, such as a gift card to a local pet store or a monetary donation made in their name to an animal shelter.

Tips for Interviewing a Potential Dog Handler

Start by meeting with the dog handler and dog without your child. Trust and honor your intuition about whether or not the handler and dog will be a good fit. Try a few exercises to assess for yourself how the dog reacts to specific situations. These should include brushing the dog, offering a treat, and putting the dog through some basic commands.

Questions to ask the handler:

- ❑ Is your dog comfortable around children?
- ❑ How would you describe your dog's temperament?
- ❑ Have you helped a child overcome their fear of dogs before?
- ❑ Has your dog had obedience training? If so, for how long?
- ❑ Do you have good control over your dog?
- ❑ Are there things we need to avoid doing with your dog?

For example, some dogs don't like being petted on their heads while others are sensitive near their tails. If the dog you're working with has preferences like these, make sure the child avoids these interactions. Some dogs may become agitated if a frightened child screams or tries to run away. Obviously, a dog that reacts poorly to a fearful child would not be a good choice for this therapy.

THE ROLE OF THE DOG
Understanding the Role of the Dog

It's important to choose the right dog to assist in the OFOD Protocol to ensure that things go well.

Use the checklist below to help you choose the right dog for your child's therapy exercises.

Checklist for Choosing the Right Dog

- ❑ Likes children.
- ❑ Has basic obedience training (sit, stay, lay down).
- ❑ Listens to its handler.
- ❑ Has a calm demeanor.
- ❑ Will not jump up on the child.
- ❑ Will not lick the child.
- ❑ Will be okay on leash during sessions.

The dog's role is to help show your child that they can feel safe around dogs. The dog must be able to remain on its leash during the entire session and must respond to basic commands from both the handler and the child. A dog that likes children, has a calm demeanor, and listens well is an ideal candidate. Most children are familiar with being told "you need to listen," which means the child is expected to behave appropriately and to follow the instructions being given by a teacher or parent. Dogs and children have a lot in common; just as children don't always listen and follow instructions perfectly, even well-behaved dogs occasionally slip up.

> **Once in a while, Fozzie will decide he's tired of sitting on cue or he will paw at my treat bag. When this happens, I ask the child, "Is Fozzie being a good listener?" This always gets the child's attention, and they usually smile or chuckle about this. Then we work together to get Fozzie's attention again.**

Most dogs know a trick or two, and some know many tricks. Fozzie can "give a paw," catch a tossed treat, roll over, and do a "high five," among others. Tricks are fun, but they aren't mandatory for participating in the exercises. As long as the dog will obey commands and stay in one place — either sitting or lying down — so the child can approach and eventually pet the dog, this is good enough.

When the child is giving the dog commands, the handler may need to use hand signals to reinforce the verbal commands to make sure the dog obeys. Fozzie knows the verbal commands for sit, down, and stay, but I also use hand signals. This way, the child can use a vocal command and I can reinforce it with a hand signal. Most children don't pick up on the hand cues in the beginning because they don't take their eyes off the dog. It gives the child a giant boost of confidence when the dog does what the child is asking. I will usually reinforce this progress by saying, "You're a dog trainer! Fozzie is listening to you."

Puppies are adorable and many children (and adults) will be drawn to them, but they are unpredictable. Puppies are not a good choice for structured exposure sessions, as they tend to be energetic, jumpy, vocal, and not yet trained. For this reason, most therapy dog organizations have a rule that dogs need to be at least a year old before they can be evaluated for work as therapy dogs. Using a puppy for the exercises might worsen your child's fear. If all goes well, you may eventually be able to introduce a puppy to your child.

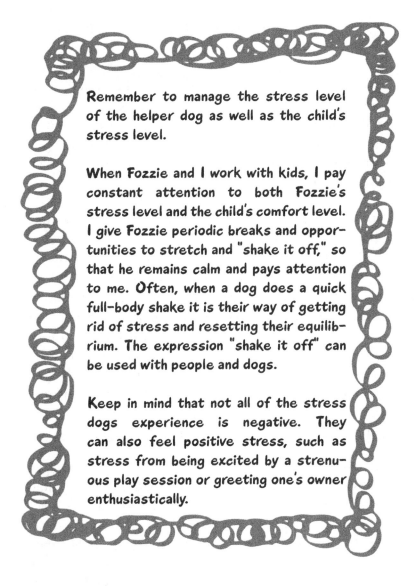

Remember to manage the stress level of the helper dog as well as the child's stress level.

When **Fozzie** and I work with kids, I pay constant attention to both **Fozzie's** stress level and the child's comfort level. I give **Fozzie** periodic breaks and opportunities to stretch and "shake it off," so that he remains calm and pays attention to me. Often, when a dog does a quick full-body shake it is their way of getting rid of stress and resetting their equilibrium. The expression "shake it off" can be used with people and dogs.

Keep in mind that not all of the stress dogs experience is negative. They can also feel positive stress, such as stress from being excited by a strenuous play session or greeting one's owner enthusiastically.

For most sessions, Fozzie remains in a lying down or sitting position most of the time. This way the child can observe him and not feel threatened. The goal is for the child to eventually be able to touch and pet him. Giving Fozzie a break during therapy sessions is important for the same reasons that having a break helps the child. Giving the dog frequent breaks helps ensure that the dog will not get too bored or stressed by the exercises.

Another meaningful canine body movement to be aware of is yawning. Most humans yawn because they're feeling sleepy. However, when a dog yawns, he is trying to communicate. "Dogs yawn as a response to stress, as a communication signal toward other dogs and/or in empathy (or at least in response to) their humans," according to PetMD.com.[9]

When I take Fozzie for a walk to give him a break, I use the time as an opportunity to have the child observe Fozzie. I engage the child by asking questions such as "what shape are Fozzie's ears?" (Triangle ☺). Then I point out that different dogs have differently shaped ears and tails. I may point out that Fozzie's tail sits curled up on his back, but Labradors and Golden Retrievers have strong tails that hang down in the back. You can give children homework assignments to research dogs and look at the shapes of their ears and tails. This is another way of desensitizing kids to dogs, by engaging their brains in thinking about other aspects of dogs so that they forget to be scared of them briefly.

What Happens if You Choose an Unsuitable Dog?

Ten-year-old Scott only needed one session to move through the protocol exercises. He became comfortable with Fozzie very quickly. We agreed that Scott was ready to interact with another dog. He wanted to try with his best friend's dog, Donovan, a one-year-old Labradoodle. Scott's mother said she would arrange it. She then let me know we could meet with Donovan the following day. As it turns out, they were squeezing us in on the same day they were planning to go on vacation. The situation felt rushed, but Scott's mother said he was excited and willing to go.

When we arrived at the Warren home, Mrs. Warren was trying to get Donovan onto a leash. The dog was running around the kitchen and not cooperating. I instructed Scott to wait outside so I could meet the dog first. Donovan had frenetic puppy energy, and as far as I could tell, no formal training. I should have honored my instincts, which told me that Scott's current comfort level was not up to meeting Donovan. Scott had been able to interact with Fozzie who was well-behaved and under my control at all times. Donovan, on the other hand, seemed to have very high energy and his owner did not seem to have much control over him.

How you can prevent getting into a situation like this:

When I'm not working with Fozzie or another dog I know well, I meet the dog ahead of time. If that isn't feasible, I have an in-depth phone conversation with the dog's owner before we schedule a session. During this screening, I pay attention to the dog's temperament:

- ❑ Is the dog mellow, "wild," or somewhere in between?
- ❑ Does the dog know some basic commands?
- ❑ Is the dog interested in being petted or brushed?
- ❑ Does the owner have thorough knowledge of the dog's behavior and good control over the dog?
- ❑ How is your dog with children?
- ❑ Will he be okay on a leash?

Unfortunately, due to the rushed timing of this session, and my (misplaced) trust in the description of the "sweet Labradoodle," I had not asked these questions or met with Donovan beforehand.

Mrs. Warren eventually leashed Donovan, after chasing him around the kitchen a few times, and we took the dog outside. Mrs. Warren had little control over the dog. The dog pulled at the leash, bounced around, jumped up on her and Scott's mother, and lunged toward Scott. This was a friendly gesture on Donovan's part, but it set back Scott's progress quite a bit. He screamed, described his fear as being back at a 10, and said he wanted to run away from the dog. But he remembered that running was one of the things you never do because the dog might chase you.

I was uncomfortable working with an uncontrolled dog, so I stopped the session after about ten minutes. This case is a reminder of how important it is to *always* screen a dog before introducing it to a child who is afraid of dogs. I also tuned in to my own feelings of discomfort around an uncontrolled and unpredictable dog, which helped me empathize with Scott and other children who are afraid of dogs.

The experience made me realize that no matter how motivated and in a hurry a child may be to overcome their fear, I always need to do my homework. When I spoke with Scott afterwards, I apologized for not meeting with Donovan first and validated his fearful feelings about this dog. I shared with him that I also felt nervous around the dog, and this seemed to help him feel better. After that, we used Fozzie's friend Charlie for a session. Charlie is a small three-year-old Shi Tzu who is very docile. Following this session, Scott was able to be close to and interact with predictable dogs on leashes. To safeguard Scott's progress, we all agreed that for the foreseeable future, whenever he went to his best friend's house, Donovan needed to be kept in a separate room.

In the next chapter, you will learn about the Overcoming the Fear of Dogs Protocol (OFOD) and how to apply it. I developed this method to help my daughter overcome her fear of dogs and have been using it to help other children for over 25 years.

Chapter 5:
The Protocol for Overcoming The Fear of Dogs

"You are braver than you believe
Stronger than you seem
Smarter than you think
And loved more than you'll ever know"
— A.A. Milne, *Winnie the Pooh*

This chapter will teach you the method I use to help children who are afraid of dogs to become less afraid of them. By using exposure therapy and the exercises I have designed, you will gradually decrease your child's fear and resistance. Our ultimate goal is to enable children to be comfortable around dogs and even interact with them.

In this chapter, you will learn:

- What exposure therapy is and how to use it to alleviate your child's fear of dogs
- The steps of my fear-reduction protocol and how to complete them
- How the protocol has worked for other children
- By filling out the questionnaire I designed, you will better understand your child's fear of dogs and how it developed

Desired Outcomes/Goals

When your child overcomes fear, they gain:

- ❑ Self-confidence
- ❑ Self-esteem
- ❑ Respect
- ❑ An ability to cope with anxiety and fear
- ❑ The confidence to speak up about what they need
- ❑ Greater awareness of their feelings

EXPOSURE THERAPY

"Exposure therapy is a psychological treatment that was developed to help people confront their fears. When people are fearful of something, they tend to avoid the feared objects, activities or situations. Although this avoidance might help reduce feelings of fear in the short term, over the long term it can make the fear become even worse. In such situations, a psychologist might recommend a program of exposure therapy in order to help break the pattern of avoidance and fear. In this form of therapy, psychologists create a safe environment in which to 'expose' individuals to the things they fear and avoid. The exposure to the feared objects, activities or situations in a safe environment helps reduce fear and decrease avoidance."

Source: American Psychological Association (APA) Clinic Practice Guideline for the Treatment of Post-traumatic Stress Disorder

When working with exposure therapy, it is helpful to understand what it is and why it is used for treating anxiety and phobias. Exposure therapy involves starting with more benign and less threatening situations that help an individual confront their fears in a manageable way. The goal is to gradually build the person's confidence so they can handle more frequent and longer exposures to the situation that generates their fear. Exposure therapy is the best approach to help children overcome their fear of dogs. When using this technique to treat a child's fear of dogs, the child's fears will gradually diminish as their exposure to well-behaved dogs increases.

My hope for fearful children is for them to at least tolerate being near dogs. My goal is that they will eventually learn to like dogs and be able to enjoy the benefits of interacting with them. Through the Overcoming Fear of Dogs (OFOD) Protocol, you will learn more about your child's fear, which will help you understand their feelings and plan safe exposures to dogs. Exposure therapy uses a hierarchy technique of gradually increasing exposures, such as moving from viewing pictures and videos of dogs to interacting with real dogs. My protocol outlines these steps for you.

As parents and caregivers, we feel a responsibility to protect kids and keep them safe. If we allow children to avoid dogs at all costs, we are sending them the message that dogs are scary and that they are right to be afraid. By demonstrating that you understand their fear, while at the same time insisting gently but firmly that they learn how to cope with their feelings about spending time with dogs, we can help them gradually feel less afraid and more comfortable around dogs.

I know from years of experience that the best way to help children overcome their fear is to recognize it, acknowledge it, make a plan, and implement that plan with the child as a willing participant.

THE OVERCOMING FEAR OF DOGS PROTOCOL (OFOD)

I designed the OFOD Protocol based on the principles of exposure therapy, a proven technique for treating phobias. Through exposure therapy, you gradually increase your child's interactions with dogs and desensitize them to the fear they currently associate with dogs. The exposures need to be consistent, frequent, and spaced as closely together as possible.

Things to keep in mind as you go through the steps:

Remember, this protocol decreases your child's fear by gradually increasing exposure and interactions with a helper dog. The more time you spend experiencing something safely, the more comfortable you will feel. The exercises in the protocol will help desensitize your child to dogs by allowing them to observe and interact with them in a safe and controlled manner.

Check in frequently with your child to reassess their level of fear and ask them how they are feeling. Pay attention to your child's body language, and when you see they are feeling more relaxed (even if it's a tiny improvement), point it out to them. This will help give them the confidence to do more.

The recommended length of each session is 30 to 45 minutes.

When planning a session, please take into account the needs of both your child and the helper dog, as the sessions can be stressful for all involved. This includes you — the parent! **It is important to find a time when you are not rushed.** I recommend that all parties do a grounding or centering exercise before the session begins. Start with a breathing exercise, then ask the participants to visualize placing everything that happened earlier in the day off to the side so that everyone can focus on the session.

Group Breathing Exercise and Affirmations for all Participants

Take five deep breaths into your belly.

After completing these five breathing cycles, repeat these affirmations:

I am safe.

I am doing my best.

I am brave.

Dogs are fun.

Dogs are my friends.

I can do it!

Don't expect the OFOD Protocol to be an immediate cure for your child's fear of dogs. Instead, view it as a teaching tool to help your child learn how to handle their emotions and situations involving dogs. Some kids have been cured after just a few sessions, while others have made progress in smaller ways. It depends on your child and your goal for each session. Some kids will get through the majority of the OFOD Protocol steps in one day, but others may get stuck on a particular step for a few sessions. The pace should be adjusted to fit your child's needs, whatever they may be.

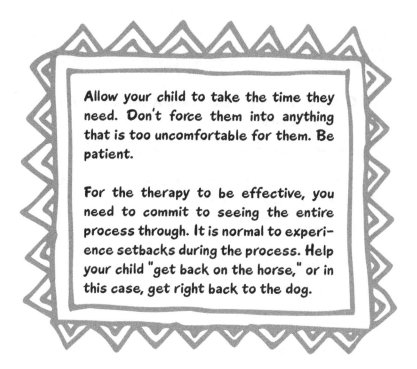

Allow your child to take the time they need. Don't force them into anything that is too uncomfortable for them. Be patient.

For the therapy to be effective, you need to commit to seeing the entire process through. It is normal to experience setbacks during the process. Help your child "get back on the horse," or in this case, get right back to the dog.

Duration and frequency of sessions

It is most helpful to have one or two sessions a week. This allows time to integrate the experience by talking about it and "re-living" it, which continues to help the child become desensitized to dogs. In between sessions, speak about the experience in a positive way, pointing out that it was fun and reinforcing your child's courage. Sessions should be no more than 45 minutes. For some children, 30 minutes will be enough. For very frightened children, you can break the session into 10-minute chunks with breaks in between while you continuously evaluate how things are going. Some children will only be able to tolerate 10 minutes of session time in the beginning. This is okay. You need to go at the child's pace. It's important to end on a positive note, therefore, end before the child becomes tired or disinterested.

When scheduling the session with a helper dog and its handler, remember that the handler knows their dog best. Avoid days when the dog has been to the vet, groomer, or has experienced other stressful situations. It is best to schedule your sessions when you have time before and after and are not pressured timewise.

While you may not always feel successful as you go through the OFOD Protocol, try to stay positive and not get discouraged or backtrack. Don't lose sight of your end goal. Your child's sense of accomplishment and pride in overcoming this emotional hurdle will be well worth it.

Before you start working with the OFOD Protocol, determine what motivates your child so you can reward them at the end of each session. Some parents may be tempted to hold out for a big reward such as a trip to the zoo. However, for behavioral reinforcement to work in this case, you need to reward after each session. In some cases, small rewards throughout the session may be necessary as well. Depending on the age of the child, stickers, small candies, screen time, etc., are all rewards that my clients have found helpful.

Remember to check in with your child about their fear level frequently. A good guideline is to ask your child to identify what number on the Fear Scale they are experiencing between each exercise. I use 1 to 10 with 1 being totally relaxed and 10 being totally panicked. When working with younger children, you can ask them instead to identify their fear as small, medium, or big.

The Fear Scale

10 — Terrified

9

8 — Very Afraid

7

6 — Moderate Fear

5

4 — Concerned & Worried

3

2 — Not Sure

1

0 — Relaxed & Comfortable

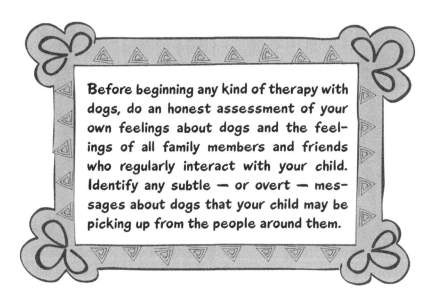

Before beginning any kind of therapy with dogs, do an honest assessment of your own feelings about dogs and the feelings of all family members and friends who regularly interact with your child. Identify any subtle — or overt — messages about dogs that your child may be picking up from the people around them.

THE OFOD PROTOCOL STEPS

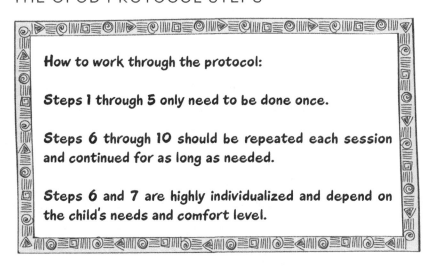

How to work through the protocol:

Steps 1 through 5 only need to be done once.

Steps 6 through 10 should be repeated each session and continued for as long as needed.

Steps 6 and 7 are highly individualized and depend on the child's needs and comfort level.

Step 1
Assess and evaluate your child's fear of dogs.

It is very important to gather as much information as possible about your child's fear to determine how you can best help them. While the following questions will help you determine where and when the fear developed, the OFOD Protocol will remain the same no matter how the fear came to be. These exploratory questions help you assess your child's concerns and understand the specifics of their fear. When you begin to explore your child's fear with the following framework, you are beginning the exposure therapy by talking about dogs.

 QUESTIONNAIRE

Note: Whenever possible, your child should actively participate in answering these questions.

1. At what age did your child's fear of dogs begin?_____

2. Did your child have a specific negative experience with a dog?
If yes, get as much information about the experience as possible.

_____

3. Did your child see a specific negative experience involving a dog happen to someone else?
If yes, get as much information about the experience as possible.

_____

4. Did your child hear about an incident involving a dog that happened to someone else?
If yes, get as much information about the experience as possible. ____

_____

5. Does your child observe you or another trusted adult being nervous around dogs?
If so, list whom and how. _____
_____

6. Did your child develop a strong fear of dogs without an obvious triggering event or cause?_____

7. Does your child have other fears?
If so, what are they?_____

8. Would you characterize your child as being anxious in general?
_____

9. How motivated is your child to overcome their fear of dogs? Very, somewhat, or not really? _____

10. Would you classify your child's fear of dogs as mild, moderate, or severe? _____

11. How would you describe your child's personality? Outgoing, reserved, slow to warm up, or timid? _____
_____

12. Does your child ask a lot of questions? Do they have a vivid imagination? _____

13. Is your child highly observant and/or extra cautious? _____
_____

It is helpful to know what causes your child to be afraid of dogs. This can be behavior dogs exhibit when meeting the child, just regular dog behavior, or the size of the dog.

Examples of common specific fears involving dogs include:

- ❑ Being licked
- ❑ Being jumped on
- ❑ Being chased
- ❑ Being bitten
- ❑ The size of the dog
- ❑ Barking
- ❑ Getting sick from dog germs
- ❑ The dog looking at them

Step 2
Assemble your team.

Your team will consist of your child, yourself or surrogate helper, a suitable dog, and the dog handler. Many parents step up as the "team leader," but you need to be comfortable around dogs for this to be successful. If you feel you may pressure your child too much or can't tolerate watching your child feel scared, then somebody else would be a better fit. A close friend or relative may be a good option. You can also consider working with a licensed therapist who is familiar with children, anxiety, and dogs.

Step 3
Begin to desensitize your child to dogs by exposing them to pictures and videos.

By looking at photos and watching videos of dogs, your child will begin to see how dogs behave in safe and nonthreatening ways. Because they are not yet interacting with a real dog, they will be able to relax and learn about dogs, dog behavior, and anything specific to the breed of the helper dog you will be using. If a family member or friend has a dog, you can research the breed and find pictures of that particular dog.

Please screen all materials ahead of time to make sure they will not increase your child's fear. For example, one father I worked with made the mistake of doing a Google search of German Shepherds with his daughter. While many appropriate items came up, there were several videos of German Shepherds learning how to attack as part of their training as K-9 officers. Needless to say, this was counterproductive and compounded his daughter's fears. YouTube can be a good resource, as long as you preview each video before showing it to your child. Websites such as Petpartners.com, Tdi-dog.org (Therapy Dogs International), and Pinterest boards are good places to find pictures of therapy dogs as well. These sites show pictures of registered therapy dogs interacting with people in safe and reassuring ways.

When doing a general search, look for photos and videos of well-behaved, relaxed, and friendly dogs interacting with children. Puppies are usually a good option. I am fond of videos that show puppies and children playing together happily. Most puppies will not yet be trained enough to act as the helper dog in the actual OFOD Protocol.

The goal is to expose your child to safe and fun images of dogs to help minimize feelings of fear and resistance when meeting the helper dog. If your child can tolerate it, find real dogs you can observe from a distance. You can drive past a dog park or other area where dogs congregate. This can be a good way to desensitize your child to the sight of dogs. Or you may want to try a visual scavenger hunt: Can you see a black and white dog? Is there a dog with a red leash? For many children, this may be too stressful. If this is the case, save the game for later in the desensitization process after your child has become more comfortable with looking at dogs.

Step 4
Look at pictures and videos of the actual helper dog.

If possible, look at pictures and videos of the helper dog's daily life. Live video chats with the helper dog using your phone or tablet can be an option, too. It is a good idea to have photos of the dog eating, playing, and being petted by its people. You can add photos of the dog at the vet or the park or doing any other daily activities you think will be helpful.

The goal of this step is two-fold: (1) to desensitize your child to seeing the helper dog in a variety of situations and (2) to "humanize" the dog so that your child sees the dog doing a lot of the same daily activities that they do in their own life:

Kids eat, so do dogs.
Kids play with toys, so do dogs.
Kids go to the doctor, so do dogs.
Kids need exercise, so do dogs.

I always show pictures of Fozzie with very young children and babies so that a fearful child can see how gentle he is and perhaps think, "If a baby isn't afraid of Fozzie, maybe I don't have to be either."

Step 5
Introduce the helper dog to the child.

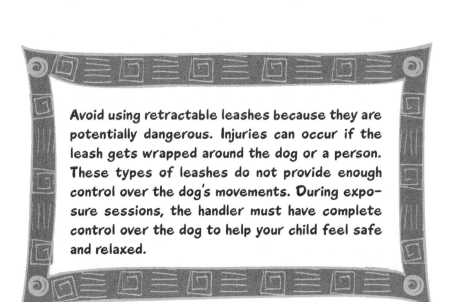

Fozzie says: Please use a leash that is six feet or shorter. Do not use a retractable leash.

Avoid using retractable leashes because they are potentially dangerous. Injuries can occur if the leash gets wrapped around the dog or a person. These types of leashes do not provide enough control over the dog's movements. During exposure sessions, the handler must have complete control over the dog to help your child feel safe and relaxed.

When you introduce your child to the helper dog, the dog must remain on a leash **at all times**. For the OFOD Protocol to be effective, your child must be able to trust that the handler has complete control over the dog. This ensures that your child can relax and participate in the session.

For very fearful children, you may want your child to view the dog from a distance at first. Weather permitting, I will sometimes keep Fozzie in the car with the window partially down so the child can view him from a distance. Another alternative is to walk the dog back and forth in the child's front yard while the child watches through the window from inside. Understand that some children need to put more space between themselves and the dog at the beginning of exposure in order to feel safe.

First impressions are key here. You want to ensure your child can manage their fear sufficiently before proceeding through the session. If the first time your child sees the helper dog it is bouncing around and acting out of control, your child will *not* want to interact with it.

Chapter Six of this book will go into more detail on the best way to introduce a child to a new dog, but below are basic guidelines to follow when introducing your child to the helper dog. These principles are also helpful when children who already enjoy interacting with dogs are meeting an unfamiliar dog for the first time.

Tips for the first meeting with the helper dog:

- ❏ Help your child to remain as calm as possible and to use their normal everyday voice.
- ❏ Don't allow your child to scream, shout, or flail their arms and legs. These behaviors may agitate even the calmest of dogs. If your child has difficulty controlling their body, voice, or emotions, give them a break to help them regain composure.
- ❏ Give your child control over how close they want to get to the dog. It may take a session or two for your child to be able to tolerate being within touching distance of the dog.
- ❏ Only approach the dog when it is stationary.
- ❏ When your child feels ready, have them move gradually closer to the dog.
- ❏ Keep in mind that how close your child can get to the dog depends on the individual child's level of fear and comfort.

❑ Once your child has accomplished being within touching distance of the dog, evaluate the most comfortable way for your child to try touching the dog.

Notes for the handler:

❑ Your dog needs to remain calm, leashed, and under your control at all times when working with the child or any time the child is nearby.
❑ Please allow your dog to eliminate before the session and, if necessary, in the middle of the session. We want the dog to be comfortable and relaxed.
❑ Periodically offer water to your dog. Kids usually find it interesting to see how dogs drink out of a water bowl. You can point out how they manipulate their tongues to lap up the water. You can also ask the child to tell you when they think the dog might be thirsty and to look for signs of thirst, such as panting or eyeing the water bowl.
❑ If the dog shows signs of stress or is not cooperating, **immediately** give the dog a break or, if necessary, stop the session altogether. It is important to consider the dog's needs as well as the child's — and a stressed-out dog will create more stress and fear in the child.

Please refer to Chapter Seven for more information about dog body language and behavior.

Step 6
Interaction with the helper dog.

Once your child has successfully met the dog, it is time to begin working together on the exposure therapy exercises.

The exercises are broken down into three types:

- ❑ **Touch exercises:** petting, brushing, placing the adult's hand on the dog and then the child's hand on the adult's hand
- ❑ **Proximity exercises:** observing the dog, standing or sitting next to the dog
- ❑ **Interaction exercises:** giving the dog a command, giving the dog a treat, giving the dog a high-five, and walking the dog

Break exercises into manageable steps.

Many children will be hesitant to jump right in and do an exercise. It may be helpful to break down each exercise into a series of less intimidating tasks. Baby steps are okay. For example, to work up to petting the dog, have your child start out by touching the dog with one finger on a spot of their choice (as long as the dog is comfortable with the chosen spot). Many children will reach out to touch the dog quickly and then pull their hand back. This is to be expected.

Gradually increase the length of time they keep their finger on the dog — such as starting with a one-second touch, then holding the finger there while counting to five and then to ten. Once your child is comfortable with the one-finger touch, you can add additional fingers until they are touching the dog with their whole hand. After your child is comfortable touching the dog with a stationary hand, you can encourage them to stroke the dog's fur — also working up to a count of ten.

Adults can model the petting exercise. Some children may want to start with their hand on top of their adult's before working up to petting and stroking the dog with their own hands.

A similar progression can be followed for brushing the dog. You can start out with the adult brushing the dog while your child holds the adult's arm. Then your child can gradually work toward holding the brush with the adult, then eventually brushing the dog by themselves for a count of ten.

Giving the dog a treat can start with your child placing their hand under the adult's hand while the adult gives the treat. This allows your child to work up to giving the dog a treat themselves.

Safety note: Not all dogs have gentle mouths. It is important to check with the handler to find out if their dog will take a treat gently and not slobber too much or grab the treat, which might result in inadvertently nipping the child's fingers. For all dogs, the best way to give a treat is to make your hand a "plate" by keeping it open and flat, with the fingers close together.

The first few times a child gives Fozzie a treat, I hold the child's hand open and flat, putting my fingers around their fingers to keep them together. It's always best to be proactive.

During these exercises, ask your child questions so that they can make direct observations, such as "Is the fur soft?" and "What color fur do you see?" This helps your child focus on something other than feeling afraid.

Recommended exercises to increase your child's desire to interact with the dog:

❑ *Put the dog in a sit or down position.*
The dog should stay this way for the majority of the first session, with a few breaks.

If the dog needs to move or take a "potty" break, tell the child that this is going to happen before you release the dog from the stay command so there are no surprises.

❑ *Ask your child to gauge their fear using the Fear Scale.*
Do this several times during the session.

❑ *Breathing.*
Make sure your child is relaxed, otherwise pause and have the child take five deep breaths. Do this periodically throughout the session.

❑ *Ask your child to tell you three things they notice about the dog.*
This could be the color of the dog's fur, how they think the dog is feeling, what shape its ears are, etc.

❑ *Ask your child to come closer to the dog.*

❑ *Model petting the dog for your child.*
Describe how the fur feels. Mention if it's as soft as you thought it would be and if it feels the same on different parts of the dog. For example, Fozzie's fur is the softest around his neck.

❑ *Brushing the dog.*
Kids who are on the verge of being willing to brush the dog can hold onto the adult's wrist while the adult brushes the dog. Eventually, your child should be encouraged to brush the dog on their own.

Step 7
Do longer exercises spaced more closely together.

As the process goes on, you should gradually decrease the time between the exercises and do each one for a longer period of time. For example, if the child starts off by petting the dog with one finger, encourage them to use three fingers, then four, then the whole hand. The goal is to have them pet the dog with the full hand without starting with one finger. If they start out petting with a quick touch, encourage them to try keeping their hand on the dog for a count of two, and then have them work up to counting to five or ten.

When working on this progression, it is important not to allow too much time between the actions because your child may become resistant. Once your child can keep their hand on the dog for a count of ten, have them repeat this several times in a row. This will reinforce your child's confidence and decrease the level of fear.

Then you can move on to petting **and** stroking the dog down their entire back. Work up to a count of ten. Do each exercise until your child's fear level is six or lower.

As we saw in Step 6, the goal is for your child to be able to continue each exercise for a little longer each time and to repeat the exercises several times in close succession. Each session should begin with a quick run-through of each exercise your child has already mastered before beginning new exercises. For example, if your child was previously able to greet the dog from a distance, ask the dog to sit and stay, and pet and brush the dog, you would start the new session by having your child do all of those things a few times before beginning the new exercise. This helps reinforce your child's confidence and allows them to start feeling comfortable. As parents, you will need to find the sweet spot of encouraging your child to move forward even though they are anxious. If you pressure or force your child to do something they are afraid to do, it will backfire.

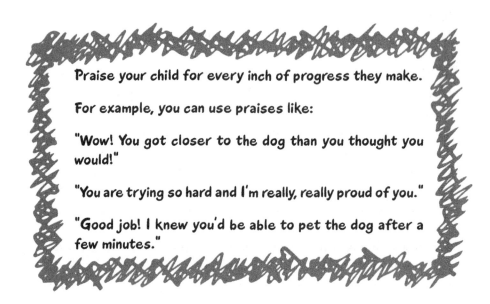

Praise your child for every inch of progress they make.

For example, you can use praises like:

"Wow! You got closer to the dog than you thought you would!"

"You are trying so hard and I'm really, really proud of you."

"Good job! I knew you'd be able to pet the dog after a few minutes."

Step 8
Repeat exercises until the fear level decreases.
Goal: Your child will learn that they *can* have control and they *can* tolerate their own strong feelings enough to face their fears.

With each exposure, your child's level of fear should go down. Within each session, there will be many opportunities to help lower your child's fear level. If they start out by petting the dog with one finger and their heart is pounding, have them take some deep breaths, say, "I can do this," and gradually work up to petting the dog with the whole hand. The more your child pets the dog and sees that it is safe, the less afraid they will feel.

Step 9
Reward your child.

If you have gotten to this step, let your child know they are a superhero!

Your child has faced their fear and deserves a lot of praise. Help your child acknowledge their bravery and success by having them repeat "I did it!" You should be praising and cheering your child on throughout each session. Most children find the process itself rewarding and they feel proud of their progress and relieved to be less afraid.

> **Remember to praise and encourage your child during every exercise and reward them at the end of each session.**

You can take a picture of your child with the helper dog and text it to Grandma or another close family member. Please get your child's permission first so they can continue to feel in control and trust the process. I have yet to meet a child who doesn't want to share their progress with loved ones. If you have offered your child a reward for achieving a specific goal, such as stickers, ice cream, or an hour to spend playing a favorite video game, be sure to deliver on your promise. Your child needs to know that you will follow through on what you promise.

I use a certificate, which is a good motivator. The certificate includes several boxes to check as your child completes each exercise. After your child accomplishes the first checkbox goal, "Being near a dog," we work up to "Walking a dog."

"I am brave with dogs!"

This certificate hereby declares that

_____

gets a gold star for:

- ❏ Being near a dog
- ❏ Petting a dog
- ❏ Brushing a dog
- ❏ Giving a dog a treat
- ❏ Shaking a dog's paw
- ❏ Walking a dog

...but mostly for being
BRAVE AND KIND!

_____

(adult signature)

When your child has completed all the steps and all the boxes have been checked, they get to keep the certificate. Some families frame their children's certificates and hang them on the wall to show their kids how proud they are of them. I even have a superhero cape with the words Captain Pawsitive on it and I take a picture of the child wearing it standing next to Fozzie. The smiles say it all!

Step 10
Review.

After each session, fill out the Exercise Log. This will provide an opportunity to assess what went well, what needs more reinforcing, and what your goals are for the next session. Please refer to the Resource Section for a copy of the exercise log.

By reviewing each session, you will be able to hone in on your child's progress and any areas that need more attention. Remember that each child's rate of progress will be different. With some, you will celebrate baby steps, such as the child being able to stand five feet away from the dog instead of being in the other room. With others, you may get through the steps quickly and the child will graduate to interacting with other dogs in less-controlled situations.

Irina's Story, Age Nine

Nine-year-old Irina was deathly afraid of all dogs. She played soccer and often parents and other spectators would bring leashed dogs to her team's practices and games. If there was a dog near the field, even on a leash, Irina wasn't able to concentrate on playing soccer. Instead, she kept her eyes on the dog, and if she felt it was getting too close, she would run away. Irina was a rare case. She was never able to come closer to Fozzie than about eight feet away. We did four sessions in her house, and Irina felt the need to stay at the top of the stairs or at the far end of the room whenever I had Fozzie with me. We made an agreement that I would not bring him close to her, as long as she continued to have him in her sight. I put Fozzie through his paces, having him sit, stay, lie down, and high-five me on command — all with Irina watching from a distance.

Although Irina wasn't interacting directly with Fozzie, she was experiencing being near a live dog and learning about dog behavior. Her friend Marlee joined the session once, and Irina watched Marlee interact with Fozzie directly. Marlee went through all the exercises on the certificate and tried to coax Irina to come closer to the dog.

Irina's mother reported that, while she was never able to get any closer to Fozzie, she was able to play soccer with a dog nearby. We also let Irina know that if there was a dog running loose, she could ask the owner to put it on a leash, since that was the rule at the park where her soccer games were held. We did some role-playing during our sessions to help her feel comfortable approaching dog owners. She practiced asking that a dog be leashed.

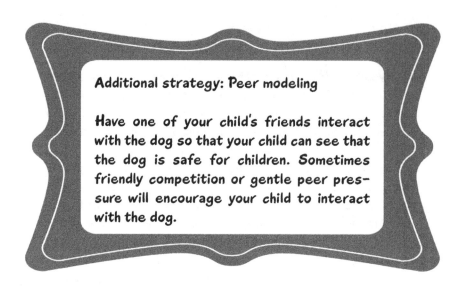

Additional strategy: Peer modeling

Have one of your child's friends interact with the dog so that your child can see that the dog is safe for children. Sometimes friendly competition or gentle peer pressure will encourage your child to interact with the dog.

CASE STUDY: RYAN, Age 8

This case study is intended to help you better understand the OFOD Protocol and each individual step.

Step 1: We assessed and evaluated Ryan's fear.

I met Ryan in the fall of 2017. His mother contacted me after he refused to go to a birthday party at a friend's house where there was a resident dog. Ryan was eight years old at the time. I began by gathering information on Ryan's fear of dogs by asking the following questions:

Depending on the age of your child and their willingness to participate, these questions should be posed to the child. If the child needs help answering them, the parent can jump in.

QUESTIONNAIRE

1. At what age did your child's fear of dogs begin and/or when did you first notice it?

As far as Ryan's parents could remember, Ryan had always been afraid of dogs. Ryan agreed that he has always been afraid. When Ryan was in preschool, his parents noticed that whenever they encountered a dog, Ryan would become upset and ask to be picked up.

2. Did your child have a specific negative experience with a dog? If yes, get as much information about the experience as possible.

Ryan's parents did not think so and Ryan agreed.

3. Did your child see someone else have a negative experience involving a dog? If yes, get as much information about the experience as possible.

Ryan said no.

4. Did your child hear about an incident involving a dog that happened to someone else? If yes, get as much information about the experience as possible.

Ryan said no.

5. Does your child observe you or another trusted adult being nervous around dogs? If so, whom and how?

Bingo! No one in Ryan's immediate family had had any relevant experiences with animals, positive or negative. However, both his parents used extreme

caution around dogs. They denied feeling afraid, but Ryan may have picked up on their hypervigilance around dogs and interpreted it as fear. For example, if they saw a dog, they would cross the street to be on the opposite side. They never encouraged Ryan or his younger sister to interact with dogs. Through our discussion, Ryan's mother realized that she may have been responding to Ryan's tentativeness around dogs by avoiding them altogether.

6. Did your child develop a strong fear of dogs without an obvious triggering event or cause?

For Ryan, the answer was YES.

7. Does your child have other fears? If so, what are they?

According to his parents, and Ryan agreed, Ryan is generally outgoing and does not have other fears that paralyze him the way his fear of dogs does. He sleeps with a night light and occasionally has nightmares, but this is well within the norm for children his age.

8. Would you characterize your child as being anxious in general?

All agreed, Ryan is not an anxious child.

9. How motivated is your child to overcome their fear of dogs? Very, somewhat, or not really?

Ryan said he wanted to overcome his fear because it was starting to impact his ability to spend time with his friends. He added that he was starting to feel embarrassed by his fear. We categorized him as **VERY** motivated.

10. Would you classify your child's fear of dogs as mild, moderate, or severe?

Together we determined Ryan's fear was somewhere between moderate and severe. His fear of dogs was now preventing him from doing things other eight-year-old boys enjoyed.

11. How would you describe your child's personality? Outgoing, reserved, slow to warm up, or timid?

Ryan's parents described him as a healthy and active eight-year-old who was an above-average student. Ryan added that he liked school and was comfortable participating in class discussions.

12. Does your child ask a lot of questions? Do they have a vivid imagination?

Ryan's parents described him as curious and bright and said he often created elaborate buildings with Legos. Through our discussions, Ryan's parents realized that he did ask a lot of questions before having a new experience. For example, one summer the family participated in a family reunion in the Poconos. His mom said he asked a million questions; "Who will be there? Where will I sleep? How many bathrooms are there? Is there a heated pool? A game room? Will anyone have a dog?" Ryan added that he liked to be "prepared."

13. Is your child highly observant and/or extra cautious?

Ryan's parents noted that he had a very good memory and often remembered details that other people did not. For example, he often noticed small details in book illustrations that others missed. This helped me realize that he was an observant child. This is important to note because children often see and observe things they have no point of reference for yet and won't fully understand until they are older or experience them directly. This can feed anxiety and worry.

14. What specifically is your child afraid of?

Ryan told me that he was afraid of dogs in general. He definitely did not want to be licked or jumped on.

From the answers on the questionnaire, we learned that Ryan had developed his fear of dogs primarily through an *instructional* experience. He had observed his parents acting very cautiously around dogs and he was never afforded the opportunity to interact directly with dogs. As a result, he felt unsure around them, which developed into cynophobia. Ryan also had the type of temperament that lends itself to the *personality* type of fear development. He was very observant, imaginative, and bright. Because he had no real experiences with dogs, his imagination led him to believe that they were dangerous. When pressed, Ryan was able to state specifically that he did not want to be licked or jumped on. We also learned that Ryan was very motivated to overcome his fear because it was starting to affect his social life.

> **Always pinpoint the specifics of your child's dog-related fears.**

Step 2: We assembled our team.

Our team consisted of Ryan, Sharon (Ryan's mother), Fozzie, and me. We also occasionally included Ryan's younger sister Sophia in the process. While Sophia had not had many experiences with dogs, she was not afraid of them. We used her to help model that Fozzie was a safe dog to be around.

Step 3: We familiarized Ryan with dogs.

Even though Ryan was afraid of dogs, he was interested in learning about them. He was particularly interested in some of the work that dogs can do. We looked for photos and videos of dogs doing a variety of tasks. Every day, Ryan and his dad spent ten minutes watching pre-screened dog videos online.

In addition, I had Ryan do some supervised research (this was to make sure he did not come across any inappropriate or frightening material) on assistance and therapy dogs — such as dogs that help sense a seizure or diabetic episode before it happens. We also saw drug-sniffing dogs working at airports and dogs being read to by children at libraries. He took a special liking to herding dogs, such as Australian Shepherds and Border Collies. He learned as much as he could about these two breeds. In doing so, he was flooded with pictures of dogs and information about them, which began the process of desensitizing him to dogs.

Ryan told us that he did not yet feel comfortable looking at real dogs, and we respected this. I said that would be a future goal. By providing children with goals, you are demonstrating that you have confidence in their ability to overcome their fears.

During this step, you can also begin to familiarize your child with dog body language and what a relaxed, friendly dog looks like. Chapter Six goes into more detail on this and there are more suggestions in the Resource Section of this book.

Step 4: We looked at photos and watched videos of the helper dog (Fozzie).

Because we were using my dog Fozzie as the helper dog, I was able to show Ryan lots of photos and videos of him. I made sure to show Ryan videos of Fozzie interacting with other children so Ryan would begin to realize that Fozzie was a safe and fun dog to be around. I asked Ryan to do some research on Fozzie's breed (Keeshond). I also asked him to come up with three things he wanted to ask me about Fozzie. His questions were: "Where does Fozzie sleep?" "What is he saying when he barks?" and "Will he come near me if I don't want him to?" Because Ryan had become an expert on Australian Shepherds and Collies, we were able to talk about how Fozzie's breed, Keeshond, was different from the herding breeds. Keeshonden are bred to be companion dogs and they are in the non-sporting category at dog shows. They are originally from the Netherlands and were bred to accompany their owners on barges. Their nickname is "Smiling Dutchman."

It's important to note that we worked through four steps of the protocol before Ryan began interacting with a real dog. This shows how important it is to go at the child's pace; Ryan needed quite a bit of exposure to dogs in pictures and videos before he felt comfortable enough to meet Fozzie. Other children may need less virtual exposure to dogs before working with one in person, and some may need even more time with photos and videos before meeting the helper dog.

Step 5: We introduced Fozzie to Ryan.

After some discussion with Sharon, we decided it would be best to work in the family's finished basement. Fozzie and I entered the basement through the attached garage. Fozzie remained on his leash and close to my side. Ryan ran to his room as soon as he knew we were in the house. After some coaxing, we were able to get Ryan to sit in the kitchen, at the top of the stairs to the basement, looking down at Fozzie about twelve stairs away. Ryan said his fear level was at a ten and that his heart was pounding. We asked him to take some deep breaths, counting to four with each breath in and out.

I asked Ryan if he trusted me, and he said yes. I assured him that he would not be forced to do anything he didn't want to do. This drives home the importance of developing a relationship with the child before a dog is introduced. I had met with Ryan one time by myself without Fozzie to establish a trusting relationship. Some children are more guarded and resistant and it will take a few sessions before they trust me well enough to proceed.

I put Fozzie through his paces — sit, lie down, stay. I had Ryan tell Fozzie to sit (I also gave Fozzie a hand signal). Fozzie obliged, and then I told Ryan it was hard for Fozzie to hear him (wink, wink), and asked if he could please come down a few steps. He agreed to come down to the sixth step and said he'd like his mom to sit there with him. Ryan was now close enough to see Fozzie fairly well. I asked him to tell me three things he noticed about Fozzie. Ryan said he noticed that Fozzie was very furry and that his ears were triangular. He couldn't think of a third observation, so I asked him how he thought Fozzie was feeling. We referred to a handout on dog body language, and Ryan said Fozzie looked relaxed. I agreed.

Periodically throughout our session, I asked Ryan to describe his fear level on a scale of one to ten. When it got to a six, I asked him if he was ready to come off the steps and sit on the couch. He emphatically said no and actually ran back up to the top of the steps. This is typical behavior. **You will probably find that for every step the child takes forward, there may be one or two steps backwards**.

I reminded him that we would not make him sit on the couch until he was ready — but that he needed to come back to the sixth step. He took a few more deep breaths to calm down and eventually was able to return to the sixth step. I had him give Fozzie some commands to sit and lie down. This helped Ryan feel empowered and in control. We ended the first session with Ryan still sitting on the sixth step, but his fear level had come down to a five. I let him know that we would meet again in three days and told him we would begin the session on the sixth step, but that he would quickly work his way closer to the dog because I had confidence in him and I knew he was brave.

Ryan's homework was to continue to research friendly, well-behaved dogs and to draw a picture for Fozzie. I suggested to his mom that she talk about how proud she was of him and reinforce how brave he had been. I also suggested that she call some relatives and tell them about the session and let Ryan overhear the conversation.

Steps 6 to 9: Ryan interacted with Fozzie.

When Ryan's second session began, he wanted to be at the top of the stairs again. I reminded him that our deal was that he would start at the sixth step. He agreed but said his fear level was at an eight. I asked him to do more deep breathing, then I had him do the following grounding exercise:

> *Start by paying attention to how your feet feel on the floor, and then use each of your other senses to notice things around you.*

Ryan said he *heard* the television upstairs, could *feel* the carpeted stairs with his fingers, *saw* a big fluffy dog, *tasted* the ice cream he had been promised, and *smelled* his sister's bad breath. Ryan had a fun sense of humor, and these last two comments about tasting ice cream and smelling his sister's bad breath gave us an important opportunity to laugh and break some of the tension he was feeling. Ryan's mother was also feeling a little nervous, and the humor helped her relax also. After the grounding exercise, Ryan said he was ready to move to the third stair.

I asked Ryan if he noticed anything different about Fozzie from the last time. Fozzie was wearing a patterned collar instead of his regular purple collar, but his fluffy fur made it hard to see. This was a subtle way to get Ryan to look more closely at Fozzie, and even to come down a few steps closer to him. Ryan exclaimed that the collar had paw prints on it. I casually pointed out that he was now closer to Fozzie and that he should feel very proud. Ryan smiled and said his fear level was at a five. I then had Ryan give Fozzie the commands to sit and lie down again.

I remarked on how well Ryan was doing and pointed out that Fozzie was less nervous today, too. I explained to Ryan that Fozzie knew that Ryan was a kind boy, just like Ryan knew that Fozzie was a friendly dog. Whenever possible, it is good to remind kids that dogs have feelings and are a lot like children in many ways.

Ryan needed a lot of reassurance that I would not let Fozzie lick him or jump on him. I kept Fozzie fairly stationary, either lying down or sitting, so Ryan could relax. Our goal for this session was for Ryan to get close to Fozzie. I continued to check in with Ryan about his fear level and it stayed at about five for most of the session. Ryan's mother promised him ice cream if he could come off the steps and go sit on the couch. I am not opposed to using rewards to help motivate children to work through their fears, especially if they are effective for that particular child.

Ryan did succeed in making it off the steps and walking very quickly to the couch, but I needed to keep Fozzie on a tight leash at the other end of the room. With some prodding, Ryan agreed to let me bring Fozzie closer to him while he sat on the couch. Ryan told Fozzie to sit, and we talked about something unrelated to dogs. I asked him about a soccer camp he would be going to in the summer. His eyes lit up and he told me about the scrimmage games he had played and that he was a pretty good player.

This conversation served as a break in the session. After a few minutes of this distraction, we turned our attention back to Fozzie. I asked Ryan if he was ready to try and brush or pet him. He gave me a firm no. I suggested that Ryan touch Fozzie with one finger. He agreed, but only if Fozzie was lying down and more interested in getting treats than looking at him. Ryan touched Fozzie with his index finger and said he was very soft. With some more coaxing, he then used his whole hand to pet Fozzie on his back. We worked up to him petting Fozzie for a count of ten. I had complete control of Fozzie during the entire exercise to make sure Fozzie stayed still.

Towards the end of this petting exercise, Ryan was beaming with pride. His body was more relaxed, and I asked him if he wanted to try brushing Fozzie now. He was hesitant, so we had his mother hold the handle of the brush while Ryan held onto her arm. In this way, they brushed Fozzie together, and Ryan continued to smile throughout the process. This was as far as Ryan was comfortable going that day, so we agreed that next time we would start with petting, then Ryan would brush Fozzie himself.

After five sessions, Ryan was much more comfortable around Fozzie and his fear level never went above a three. We thought it would be helpful for me to do a session or two with Ryan and the neighbor's dog, Clancy. Clancy was an energetic Goldendoodle who sometimes got loose and came onto Ryan's property. We wanted Ryan to feel comfortable around this dog and know what to do if Clancy came over to visit without his human.

We arranged to go to the Humphrey's home to meet Clancy on his territory. The agreement was that Clancy would stay on his leash unless Ryan indicated it was okay to take him off the leash. Clancy barked when we knocked on the door, and Ryan said his fear level was at a nine. We did some breathing exercises, along with having Ryan say out loud, "I can do it!" and "Clancy is a nice dog."

When we walked in, Ryan asked Clancy to sit, and he did! This immediately reduced Ryan's fear level because he knew that he was in control of the situation. Clancy stayed in a sitting position, and after a lot of encouragement and coaxing, Ryan was able to pet him. We felt that was enough for one day and we wanted to end on a high note. The following day, we went back and repeated the same things. After Ryan pet Clancy a few times, I asked if he was comfortable enough to have Clancy taken off his leash. He said he wasn't, so Mrs. Humphrey walked Clancy around the house, getting closer and closer to Ryan with each pass.

During this exercise, we practiced what to do if Ryan felt worried when he needed to walk past a leashed dog on a sidewalk or in a park. He learned to turn his whole body sideways, cross his arms on his chest, and look away from the dog. Doing this makes you less interesting to the dog, and the dog will hopefully find something more interesting to sniff or interact with.

We checked in with Ryan's fear level, and although it fluctuated during the session, it stayed between four and six. Remember that Ryan's original fear was of active and jumpy dogs, so it was up to the adults to make sure Clancy did not jump on Ryan. This allowed Ryan to feel more in control and less worried about being jumped on.

STEP 9: We rewarded Ryan.

Rewards need to be tailored to the individual child. Some will be happy with a high-five and verbal praise. Others may need a more tangible reward, such as a sticker, a few dollars, or a special outing. To overcome entrenched fear, you may need to up the ante and use something highly motivating. Ryan's parents were comfortable using ice cream as the reward, and it seemed to work.

I also used the certificate to help motivate Ryan to keep working his way through the hierarchy of interactions with Fozzie. We were able to check off "Being near Fozzie" after the first session and "Petting Fozzie" after the second session. Ryan wanted to check off the next box, "Brushing Fozzie," after the second session as well, but I said we'd be able to do that next time, after Ryan had brushed him without his mom's help. This provided extra motivation for him to earn another check on the certificate. Once the certificate was completely checked off, Ryan's parents framed it.

STEP 10: We reviewed Ryan's progress.

After each session, we reviewed what we had accomplished, filled out the exercise log, checked off the milestones on the certificate, and asked Ryan how he felt about the session. Ryan was visibly pleased with himself and always felt more relaxed at the end of each session than he had at the beginning of it. He said he felt relieved and proud of himself. He also said he wanted to call his grandmother and tell her all about Fozzie. We took a picture of Ryan with a giant smile standing next to Fozzie and sent it to his proud grandmother.

Brave with Dogs!

Session Log

Date of Session	10/11/17 (2nd Session)	
Participants	Ryan, age eight	Fozzie, eight-year-old male Keeshond
	Sharon, Ryan's mother	Stefani, Fozzie's handler and Licensed Social Worker
Session Duration	45 minutes	
Goals	1. Perform a *proximity exercise* by having Ryan get closer to the dog than he was last time, and have Ryan remain in the same room with the dog for the entire session (i.e., stay off the staircase). 2. Perform an *interaction exercise* by asking Fozzie to follow some commands, such as "sit" and/or "lie down." 3. Perform a *touch exercise* by petting or brushing the dog. This can be done with a parent's assistance — Ryan can hold his mother's arm or place his hand on hers while she pets the dog.	
Activities Successfully Performed with the Dog	1. Ryan got closer to Fozzie than he did during the first session, and he stayed off the staircase. 2. Ryan asked Fozzie to sit, lie down, and stay. Fozzie complied. 3. Ryan pet Fozzie — he started out using one finger and gradually worked his way up to petting Fozzie with his full hand for ten seconds! 4. Ryan brushed Fozzie by holding onto Mom's arm while she brushed. Average fear level: Four to six.	

Goals Achieved	Goal #1: Yes Goal #2: Yes Goal #3: Yes
Relaxation Exercise	Yes / No If yes, which one? **YES** – Deep breathing and mindfulness exercise: using his senses to notice what was around him. Planned distraction by discussing things unrelated to dogs for a few minutes.
Fear Scale	Beginning 6 Middle 5-6 End 4
Next Session	Ryan will begin the session off the steps and closer to Fozzie — either standing near him or sitting on the couch while Stefani brings Fozzie closer. Ryan will repeat the exercises he has already completed — telling Fozzie to sit, stay, and lie down — and he will pet Fozzie with his full hand for a count of ten. Ryan will work up to brushing Fozzie without his parent's assistance, also for a count of ten.
Goals for Ryan's Next Session	1. Begin session in closer proximity to the dog — off the staircase from the beginning. 2. Put Fozzie through sit, stay, and lie down commands. 3. Pet Fozzie for a count of ten. The above goals are repeats of activities he has already mastered. By repeating tasks he has already accomplished, Ryan is reinforcing his success and decreasing his fear and resistance. The next set of goals are new activities: 4. Brush Fozzie by holding the brush himself. 5. Toss a treat to Fozzie. Based on the previous session, we know that Ryan will most likely be able to accomplish goals four and five. If Ryan seems ready, we will add:

	6. Give Fozzie a treat directly from his hand. Maintain a fear level of four or lower throughout the session.
Reward	Two boxes checked on the certificate (being near Fozzie and petting him) and, as promised, a trip with his parents to Cold Stone Creamery for an ice cream sundae.
Date for next session:	10/14/17

As Ryan's story shows, by going at the child's pace and gently but firmly encouraging them to make more progress each time, fearful children can gradually become more comfortable around dogs. The next two chapters provide tips on how to keep kids safe around dogs, as well as a guide to understanding dog behavior and decoding dog body language. Understanding what dogs are trying to communicate can help kids and adults interact with them safely and enjoyably.

Chapter 6:

How to Interact With Dogs Safely

"I am really glad that my parents taught me the right way to pet dogs and when to be sure and leave them alone. I feel safe around my dog and am always careful when I meet new dogs."

—Jonah, age 12

Author's Note: This chapter was developed in collaboration with humane educator Cathy Malkin (who also happens to be my sister). Humane education is "the use of education to nurture compassion and respect for living things," according to the Humane Education Coalition.[10]

This collaboration was born from our joint passion to keep children and animals safe, while also introducing them to the wonders of animals. We want to ensure that they can safely experience the true magic of dogs. Throughout this chapter, Cathy will share her experience, expertise, and advice with us. Her contributions are in italics.

This chapter provides guidelines on how to stay safe around dogs.

You will learn about safety from three different perspectives:

- ❑ From the parent's perspective
- ❑ From the child's perspective
- ❑ From the dog's perspective

Children (and adults) should interact differently with dogs they are familiar with than with dogs they don't know. This chapter will explore how to teach kids an appropriate dose of caution when they are near dogs. Respect is key; help children see that they should treat a dog the same way they want to be treated.

> **Remember: Not all dogs will be as well-behaved or as gentle as the helper dog that assisted you with the OFOD Protocol outlined in Chapter Five.**

Once your child has become more comfortable around dogs, I want to make sure it stays that way as your child begins petting and playing with other dogs. Knowing how to stay safe around dogs will help the child feel less dependent on other people, which will boost their self-confidence.

Dog Bites & Prevention

> **Most dog bites are preventable if you understand how to safely interact with dogs.**

More than three quarters (77%) of all dog bites are from the family dog or dogs of relatives and friends, according to dog trainer Justine Schuurmans.[11] This is why it's essential to teach children how to interact safely with dogs, even ones they are familiar with; children need to know how to behave around the dogs they come into contact with every day.

"Many people don't think about dog bites until they happen to someone that they care about," says Lesley Zoromski, the founder and president of Kids-n-K9s[12].

Lesley is a dog trainer and retired teacher. She developed a fun and easy-to-use sticker sorting activity called *Stop, Look & Paws* to help children and parents learn how to "read" dog body language so they know whether or not it is safe to interact with a dog [see Resource Section for more information on this activity packet].

Why Dogs Bite

Dogs bite for a variety of reasons. Most dogs give warning signals to let you know that they are stressed, frightened, or feeling territorial. If you and your child are mindful of your behavior, are respectful of the dog, and understand what the dog is communicating, you should be okay.

According to Doggonesafe, a non-profit organization dedicated to dog-bite prevention through education and awareness, there are many reasons a dog may bite[13]:

- ❑ The dog is protecting puppies or a possession, such as food and water dishes.
- ❑ The dog is protecting a resting place.
- ❑ The dog is protecting its owner or the owner's property.
- ❑ The child has done something to provoke or frighten the dog (e.g., hugging the dog, moving into the dog's space, leaning or stepping over the dog, trying to take something from the dog).
- ❑ The dog is old and grumpy, is having a bad day, and has no patience for the lively behavior of a child.
- ❑ The dog is injured or sick.
- ❑ The child has hurt or startled the dog by stepping on it; poking it; or pulling its fur, tail, or ears.
- ❑ The dog has not learned to control its bite reflex and bites hard by accident when the child offers food or a toy.

- The child and dog are engaging in rough play and the dog gets overly excited.
- The dog views the child as a prey item because the child is running and/or screaming near the dog, riding a bicycle, or otherwise moving past the dog.
- The dog is of a herding breed and nips while trying to "herd" the children.

This list of reasons from Doggonesafe might seem overwhelming and disconcerting, and you may now be tempted to avoid dogs. However, if you employ good safety practices with dogs, you and your child will be able to enjoy their affection and companionship. Chapter Eight will look at the benefits of the human-animal bond, and you will see that for most people, the benefits and pleasure of spending time with our canine friends far outweigh the risks.

It's important to understand that some bites are unintentional — such as when puppies nip or nick you with their teeth because they haven't yet learned to control their mouths. An overly enthusiastic adult dog may also accidentally mouth a child's fingers when receiving a toy or treat from them.

This is why it's important to teach children how to safely give dogs treats without getting their fingers in the dog's mouth. To avoid this, I tell children to offer treats with a flat, open hand like a "plate," holding their fingers tightly together.

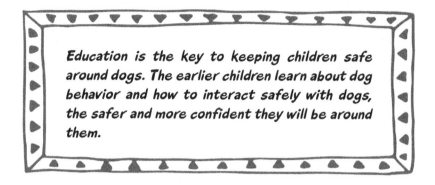

Education is the key to keeping children safe around dogs. The earlier children learn about dog behavior and how to interact safely with dogs, the safer and more confident they will be around them.

Dog safety means knowing when and how it's safe for a child to interact with dogs. Practicing dog safety involves learning dog body language, supervising your child's interactions with dogs, and teaching your child how to interact safely and respectfully with dogs. It is a common misconception that children and dogs instinctively know how to interact. Nothing is farther from the truth. It's up to adults to teach children how to read dogs' body language to make sure they interact safely and enjoyably with dogs. Many children find it empowering to be able to understand what dogs are "saying" to them and to know how to communicate with them successfully.

Throughout the process of helping your child overcome their fear of dogs, it's essential to trust your intuition: if an interaction between the dog and the child doesn't feel right, honor that feeling and intervene.

The first principle of dog safety is that a child's interactions with a dog should always be supervised by a responsible adult, even if it's the family dog. It's also up to the supervising adult to understand what to look for and recognize when it's not safe for the dog and child to interact. While you may trust your own dog around children, both dogs and children are unpredictable. It's important that an adult is always present and aware to make sure everyone stays safe.

The most important part of dog safety is educating yourself about dog behavior and how to interact safely with dogs. Once you understand how dogs communicate and respond to different situations, you can teach your children how to understand what dogs are communicating and how to treat them with kindness and respect. Please refer to Chapter Seven for more information on dog body language and behavior.

Understanding Dog Behavior Around Children

Dogs, like people, are sensitive beings who are keenly aware of the behavior, energy, and environment surrounding them and will react accordingly. Some dogs like to say hello and are friendly with new people right from the beginning. Other dogs find the presence of unfamiliar people (especially children) stressful and may react fearfully or aggressively.

Some dogs are uncomfortable meeting new people, while others may be slow to warm up to them. These sensitive dogs require extra time, patience, and space before coming into close proximity or contact with a person or child. It's important to give cautious or shy dogs time and space and allow them to interact on their own terms.

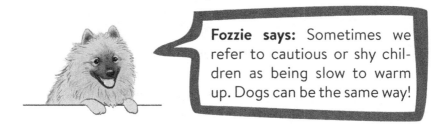

Fozzie says: Sometimes we refer to cautious or shy children as being slow to warm up. Dogs can be the same way!

Another important part of learning how to interact safely with a dog is by becoming aware of your own body language. The way you approach a dog can have a big influence on how the dog responds to you. When dogs interact with children, they can easily become anxious or afraid because of how the child is behaving. Children often behave unpredictably, and when a child feels afraid of a dog, they may scream or wave their hands, which can make dogs uncomfortable. If a frightened child runs away from the dog, the dog may give chase.

Many people don't understand or pay attention to what a dog needs when interacting with children. Parents may be so focused on what their children need or want that they aren't thinking about the dog's needs. This mindset can lead to trouble.

Many dogs will tolerate — and enjoy — human contact. However, when a dog is uncomfortable with a person's behavior and can't escape from it, they will react defensively to protect themselves. This type of pressure can lead a dog to snap or even bite.

This is why it's essential to respect dogs (and all animals) by giving them space and paying attention to their signals. Forcing a dog to cooperate with something they don't want to do, or making them remain in situations they are afraid of, is a recipe for disaster.

How Dogs Are Influenced by Our Behavior and Actions

Think about how a dog tends to mirror the behavior of its family. When a family is calmly sitting together watching TV, the dog will most likely be sitting quietly with them. If the children become excited and start running around the house, the dog will often respond by becoming excited and running around also — matching the high energy level. It's never advisable to have children interact with dogs who are overexcited, afraid, or giving signals that they want to be left alone.

Children and dogs should always be encouraged to remain calm and in control when playing together or otherwise interacting. In this way, you can help keep the dog's (and children's) behavior from getting out of control. This also applies when they're engaged in energetic activities, such as playing with a ball.

Supervision

Supervision around dogs is very important. Here's why, including some information on what you should be looking for when you're supervising kids and dogs.

It's our job as parents and caregivers to keep kids safe. The good news is that kids can safely enjoy being around dogs when they know how to interact appropriately. Most children find spending time with dogs very rewarding. During these interactions, it is important to keep both the child and the dog safe and happy.

Dog trainer Robin Bennet offers the following observations you should look out for when supervising children and dogs. In her blog post, ***Why Supervising Kids and Dogs Doesn't Work***[14], Bennet lists common dog behaviors and reactions that will help you assess interactions between children and dogs so you know when and how to intervene. We will discuss dog body language in more detail in Chapter Seven. Bennet advises us to:

❑ **Watch for loose canine body language**.
  Good dog body language is loose, relaxed, and wiggly. Look for curves in your dog's body when he is around a child. Stiffening and freezing in a dog are not good. If you see your dog tighten his body, or if he moves from panting to holding his breath (he stops panting), you should intervene. These are early signs that your dog is not comfortable.

❑ **Watch for inappropriate human behavior**.
  Intervene if your child climbs on or attempts to ride your dog. Intervene if your child pulls the dog's ears, yanks their tail, lifts the jowls or otherwise pokes and prods the dog. Don't marvel that your dog has the patience of Job if he is willing to tolerate these antics. And please don't videotape it for YouTube! Be thankful your dog has good bite inhibition and intervene before it's too late.

❑ **Watch for these three really easy to see stress signals in your dog.**
All of them indicate you should intervene and separate the child and dog:

  ❑ Yawning outside the context of waking up.
  ❑ Half-moon eye — this means you can see the whites on the outer edges of your dog's eyes.
  ❑ Lip licking outside the context of eating food.

❑ **Watch for avoidant behaviors.**
If the dog moves away from the child, intervene to prevent the child from following the dog. A dog that chooses to move away is making a great choice. He's saying, "I don't really want to be bothered, so I'll go away." However, when you fail to support his choice and allow your child to follow him, it's likely the dog's next choice will be, "Since I can't get away, I'll growl or snap to get the child to move away." Please don't cause your dog to make that choice.

❑ **Listen for growling.**
I can't believe how many times I've heard parents say, "Oh, he growls all the time, but we never thought he would bite." Dog behavior, including aggression, is on a continuum. For dogs, growling is an early warning sign of aggression. Heed it. If growling doesn't work to stop or change the child's behavior towards the dog, the dog may escalate to snapping or biting. Growling is a clue that you should intervene between the dog and the child.

Although we are focusing primarily on preventing dog bites, it is important to realize that dogs can also unintentionally hurt children by knocking them over or climbing on top of them — just as children can accidentally hurt dogs through rough play.

I trust Fozzie as much as anyone can trust a dog, but this is still not 100% because even good-natured, well-trained dogs can accidentally hurt children. For example, when my grandsons are roughhousing together, Fozzie often tries to participate by climbing on them, which might inadvertently hurt the children. To make sure this doesn't happen, I manage their interaction by removing Fozzie from the room while they're "wrestling" or by asking the boys to change how they're playing so Fozzie stays calm.

Karen's Story, Mother of Three

Karen's story illustrates the importance of supervision. Karen has three children: five-year-old twins Henry and Haley and Kevin, a three-year-old who is very active and often acts impulsively. The family also has a ten-year-old French Bulldog named Dusty, who was the couple's first "baby." Karen called me one day, very upset that the dog had nipped at one of the children. She admitted that she had not been as vigilant about supervising them as she should have been and that Kevin had put his face close to Dusty's and made some squeaky noises. Dusty had growled once, but Kevin did not stop what he was doing.

Karen heard Kevin crying loudly and went running. Kevin was not badly hurt and no skin had been broken, but he was shaken up — and so were his siblings. Karen knew that Dusty was not to blame and that she should have done a better job of supervising the children's interactions with the dog. We agreed that when she could not actively watch the children and the dog, Dusty needed to be in an exercise pen, in his crate, or in a separate room with the door closed. I told Karen that when her kids are around dogs, she needs to use the same vigilance she uses when they are in parking lots or near cars and traffic. Karen agreed, and since then she has been more careful about supervising the children's interactions with Dusty. She has also been teaching them how to read "dog," so they know how to respect Dusty's wishes when he is telling them through his body language or through a growl that he wants them to stop what they're doing. Even with some education in dog behavior, it's unrealistic to think that a child as young as Kevin will be able to control himself enough around a dog to be left unsupervised. His older siblings have more self-control, but can still get rambunctious, so Karen needs to watch them to make sure they do not fall or step on the dog accidentally.

Five Principles of Safety Around Dogs by Cathy Malkin

1. *Supervise interactions with dogs.*
   Supervise all interactions between dogs and children. Both can be unpredictable, especially when interacting with one another.

2. *Educate yourself on canine communication and body language.*

This way, you will know when it's safe for you and the child to interact with a dog.

3. **Learn the Do's and Don'ts around dogs.**
   Learn how to behave appropriately around dogs, including key Do's and Don'ts of interacting with dogs.

4. **Respect their feelings.**
   Teach children safe practices for interacting with dogs, including how to treat dogs respectfully; how to interpret dog body language and behavior, and safe practices for playing with dogs, giving them treats, etc.

5. **Trust your intuition.**

Principle #1
Supervise interactions with dogs.

> **Supervision protects both children and dogs. Familiarize yourself with how dogs communicate so you can monitor interactions effectively.**

All children, especially infants and toddlers, must be supervised around dogs, even with the family dog, because children have trouble reading dog body language. In general, children under the age of six should never be left unattended with any dog.

Many people aren't aware that dogs communicate using body language and sounds or don't know how to interpret the signals dogs give us. When dogs feel stressed, they express their feelings with a series of signals and

body language clues. Knowing how to read these signals allows you to intervene and halt the interaction before the dog becomes overwhelmed and reacts with more severe behaviors such as biting.

While a child may have good intentions around a dog, the dog may still find the child's behavior stressful or threatening. Failing to recognize the dog's warning signals can put the child at risk. Infants and toddlers are too young to know how to interact safely with animals, so you need to model appropriate behavior. This includes being kind and respectful of the dog's feelings. You must remain vigilant and aware of how both the dog and your child are behaving.

Children don't always know that touching animals in a certain way can hurt or scare them. It's your responsibility to assess a dog's body language and approachability and to make sure your child interacts with the dog in a gentle, respectful way.

With a child who is afraid or wary of dogs, it's especially important to pay attention and make sure that the child's interaction with the dog won't increase their fears. If you aren't able to monitor the interaction between the child and dog, it's safest to separate them until you do have the time and attention to observe them carefully.

Never let a child approach an unknown dog without proper adult supervision. This includes dogs belonging to a "friendly stranger," friend, or even family member. Never assume that dogs know how to interact safely with a baby — even dogs you know. Not all dogs instinctively understand what a baby is or how to behave properly around one. Therefore, it's up to the dog's owner or handler to make sure the dog understands what is expected of them and how to properly respond to their feelings of stress and anxiety in a safe manner.

Always give yourself permission to say "no" to a child, especially if they want to interact with a dog that you feel may be unsafe.

Principle #2
Educate yourself on canine communication and body language.

A dog that is safe to interact with is one who exhibits calm, polite behavior:

- *Doesn't jump, lunge, or bark excitedly*
- *Sits politely before being petted*
- *Doesn't pull to interact with you*
- *Doesn't snap or nip*

It is preferable for the dog to be sitting or lying down when you meet. Always approach a dog slowly and from the side.

Be mindful of the dog's behavior throughout the interaction. If a dog's behavior changes suddenly, halt the interaction and walk away. You can tell the child, "That's okay, maybe we'll try another time." Do not approach a dog that is lunging, barking, or acting overly excited.

When interacting with dogs, be aware of your body language and the energy you are projecting. Dogs pick up on human moods and children take their cues from adults. If you remain calm and confident, you will project calm energy to the dog, and your child will learn from you. If you are excited or nervous, you will telegraph your nervousness to the dog and your child.

Being aware of body language — your own, your child's, and the dog's — is an important part of creating safe and positive interactions with dogs. Make sure your child is calm before approaching and interacting with a dog. Dogs are sensitive and may respond negatively to an impulsive or overexcited child. Do not try to interact with a dog if your child is over-excited, crying, or yelling.

For more information about dog body language, please refer to Chapter 7.

Principle #3
Learn the Do's and Don'ts around dogs.

As mentioned before, young children don't naturally learn how to interact with dogs safely the way they learn how to walk or talk. That means it's up to parents and other caregivers to teach them about dog safety.

Learning these do's and don'ts will help children understand how to treat dogs with kindness and respect, which is the key to keeping both children and dogs safe.

- ❑ ***Do*** *use your regular tone of voice.*
- ❑ ***Do*** *stay away from sleeping dogs, eating dogs, injured dogs, elderly dogs, and parent dogs with puppies.*
- ❑ ***Do*** *ask permission from the dog's owner or handler before approaching or touching a dog.*
- ❑ ***Do*** *stand quietly with your arms by your sides when greeting a dog.*
- ❑ ***Do*** *approach a dog from the side.*
- ❑ ***Do*** *use gentle hands when touching a dog.*
- ❑ ***Do*** *stay away from the dog's mouth and any object that is in its mouth.*
- ❑ ***Do*** *ask the dog's owner or handler about the best place to touch the dog (dogs have individual preferences, just like people).*
- ❑ ***Don't*** *touch a dog on its head or hug it unless you know the dog well and are certain the dog will tolerate this.* *
- ❑ ***Don't*** *run away from a dog.*
- ❑ ***Don't*** *shout or scream. Screaming will scare the dog.*
- ❑ ***Don't*** *stare into a dog's eyes; this feels threatening to dogs.*
- ❑ ***Don't*** *tease a dog.*
- ❑ ***Don't*** *take a dog's toy or bone away.*
- ❑ ***Don't*** *put your hand inside an unfamiliar dog's fence, car window, or crate.*
- ❑ ***Don't ever*** *allow a child to put their face near any dog's face, especially when meeting a dog for the first time.*

*Once your child has overcome their fear of dogs — and if it's okay with the dog's person and, most importantly, with the dog — it may be safe to hug some dogs. Keep in mind that hugging doesn't come naturally to a dog. Some learn to accept hugs, but others don't. If a dog is uncomfortable being hugged, do **not** try to hug it. You can show the dog affection by petting it on the back or chest instead.*

Principle #4
Respecting their feelings.

Your child must learn how to behave around dogs, and the key is treating them with respect. A child who knows how to treat dogs with respect for their needs and feelings will be safer around them and will feel more confident.

When dogs feel uncomfortable being touched, they want us to back up and give them space. Sometimes our desire to pet them or our expectation that they will respond to our displays of affection just like a person would can make a dog feel uncomfortable and anxious. When dogs feel uncomfortable, they may growl or bite.

Teach children to always ask for permission of the dog's handler before approaching or petting a dog. Once you have permission, approach the dog from its side, as they find this less threatening than being approached from the front. Never allow children to sneak up on a dog, as the dog may feel threatened and respond by protecting its space.

Some human expressions of affection can make dogs uncomfortable. A common human impulse that dogs find threatening is petting the top of their head. Instead, ask the owner if the dog likes to be pet on his chest or back as most dogs prefer.

Another human behavior that dogs find threatening is hugging. Teach children to express their affection by petting dogs or giving dogs treats (with the owner's permission, of course) instead of hugging them.

It's also important for both you and your child to know when to leave a dog alone.

Principle #5
Trust your intuition.

All animals, including humans, are born with intuition. Intuition is the inner voice that tells us something important without having to go through a conscious thought process. Intuition helps keep people and animals safe and connects them with others and their environment.

"Gut feelings" or "hunches" are our intuitive nature in action. Our intuitive awareness keeps us safe by alerting us to dangerous situations. Intuition guides us on how to respond in the moment.

Andrea Deierlein, a Reiki teacher, describes intuition as an "internal GPS system." Deierlein says, "When you listen to it, it helps you know if you're going in the right direction or if you need to recalculate. Sometimes you will feel queasy or uncomfortable; this can be your intuition kicking in and telling you to change course."

As adults, we often have trouble trusting our intuition because we are socialized to believe that logic and reason are more important than feelings and hunches. Children and animals tend to be more in touch with their intuition.

When interacting with dogs and other animals, intuition can provide a very helpful indication of the animal's mood or intentions. It's important to recognize and trust those signals. For example, if you are in someone else's home and you feel uncomfortable around their dog, it's okay to ask them to put the dog on a leash or in a separate room.

> *When you're around animals, it's important to trust your feelings and intuition, even if they're in contrast to what seems logical.*

When explaining intuition to kids, I often liken it to Spider-Man's "spidey senses."

Beth's Story as an Illustration of Intuition

At Beth's home, we were discussing her concerns about her four-year-old's temper tantrums when she jumped up in the middle of a sentence and exclaimed, "I have to check the baby!" She ran upstairs and found that her 18-month-old daughter had managed to wrap the cord from the vertical blinds around her neck. The crib was placed too close to the window blinds and the baby had been able to reach them. The child wasn't making any sounds and was struggling to breathe. Beth grabbed a pair of scissors and was able to remove the cord in time, and the child was fine — thanks to her mom's intuition.

Hudson's Story is an example of what can happen when we ignore our intuition about dogs. Two-year-old Hudson was with his father at a barbeque restaurant that allowed dogs at its outdoor picnic tables. Hudson loved dogs and always wanted to pet them. A small terrier was sitting on its leash under one of the tables while his family enjoyed ribs and fries. Hudson's dad, John, asked if his son could pet the dog. The mother hesitated, then said, "I guess so." The dog was reluctant and tried to move away from Hudson, but couldn't get out of range because he was on a tight leash.

John admitted to me that he shouldn't have allowed it, but Hudson crouched down and put his face near the dog's face — a major "Don't" when interacting with dogs. The dog felt threatened and snapped at Hudson. Luckily, the dog did not bite him, and John immediately picked Hudson up and moved away quickly. Later, John realized that his instincts had been telling him not to allow Hudson to do this, but he didn't listen to it because Hudson wanted to play with the dog.

We can learn important aspects of the child-dog interaction from this example:

1. **Observation:**
   John recognized that the dog was communicating that he didn't want to interact with Hudson through his body language. He was clearly trying to back away from the interaction.

2. **Intuition:**
   John had an intuitive feeling that this was not going to go well, but he didn't act on it.

3. **Respect:**
   Hudson invaded the dog's space. Of course, a two-year-old child doesn't know better, but it's up to the adults to make sure young children respect the feelings of dogs, just as they need to respect the feelings of other children.

4. **Realistic expectations:**
   Being safe around dogs means assessing the situation carefully. Not all dogs are comfortable interacting with children at all times. In this situation, all the adults were so concerned with allowing the child to do what he wanted to do that they ignored the warning signs and allowed a situation to proceed that they knew might not have a good outcome. Hudson's dad should have listened to his instincts, and the dog's owners should have been more forceful and said something like "Our dog doesn't really like children so it's best not to pet him."

Meeting a New Dog Safely

Before approaching a dog you don't know, make sure of the following:

❑ *The dog is leashed.*
   Never try to interact with an unknown dog that is not on a leash, as it cannot be easily controlled. If an unleashed dog approaches you, stay calm and still. Don't look the dog in the eye; instead, look down or away from the dog. Fight the urge to run away. Dogs have an instinct to chase anything that runs. Doggonesafe. com, an excellent resource for bite prevention and keeping children safe near dogs, teaches children to "Be a Tree."

> **Teach Kids How to Be Safe around a Strange Dog**
> ## Be a Tree
> 1. Fold your branches (hands)
> 2. Watch your roots grow (feet)
> 3. Count in your head until the dog goes away or help comes.
>
> doggone 🐾 safe.com

□ *The dog handler has control of the dog on a loose leash.*
If the leash is held tightly, it tells you the handler may be uncomfortable or unsure of their ability to control the dog.

□ *Ask permission to pet the dog before approaching.*
If the handler says it is okay, approach the dog calmly — it is especially important with young children to make sure they don't run toward the dog.

□ *If the handler says no, don't press the issue.*
It's always safer to move on and find a dog that is receptive to interacting.

Once you have obtained permission for you and your child to interact with the dog, follow these guidelines:

□ *Don't allow a child to demand or pressure a dog (or its handler) to interact.*
Make sure the child isn't pestering the dog or trying to get it to respond. This is especially important if you see that the dog isn't responding or is displaying stress signals such as licking its lips, yawning, turning its back, or moving away from the child.

❏ *Avoid leaning directly over the dog, bringing your face or other body parts close to the dog's face, or patting the dog on the top of its head.*
These behaviors make many dogs uncomfortable, nervous, or frightened.

❏ *Observe the dog's body language.*
Use that as a guide for how to interact with him. Just as a fearful child needs to feel a sense of control during an interaction with a dog, the dog needs to feel respected and safe.

❏ *Use a calm, quiet voice.*
In general, dogs find loud or high-pitched voices upsetting. This can lead them to become overly excited or fearful and they may respond by jumping, snapping, or biting.

❏ *Avoid direct eye contact with the dog.*
Especially with dogs you don't know or have just met. Instead, look down or away from the dog until you're confident that the dog feels safe and secure.

*To a dog, direct eye con-
tact can feel threatening.
When explaining this to a child, you
can let them know it's fine to look
at the dog, just don't have a "staring contest" with the dog. Most
well-socialized dogs like **Fozzie** can
tolerate eye contact because they
have learned to accept it through
training and positive experiences
with people. Pay careful attention to
the dog's body language when you're
interacting with a new dog. If the dog
seems to be relaxed with your eye
contact, then it's okay to continue.
If the dog appears uncomfortable,
prompt the child to look down or
away from the dog.*

How to Supervise Children's Interactions with Dogs in Four Common Situations

1. **How to supervise safe interactions between your child and a dog you don't know.**

Be especially cautious and vigilant when interacting with unfamiliar dogs. Do not rely on the owner's description of the dog as friendly, especially if your intuition or the dog's behavior is telling you otherwise. If you decide that the dog is safe for your child to interact with, follow the steps outlined in *Meeting a New Dog Safely* above.

Pay attention and supervise the entire interaction. If at any point the child becomes too excited, starts playing roughly with the dog, or the dog starts jumping up, step in and stop the interaction immediately. Say "thank you" to the dog's owner or handler and guide the child away from the dog. If the dog becomes overexcited or exhibits signs of stress or aggression, place your body between the dog and your child and calmly move your child away from the situation.

2. **How to supervise safe interactions between your child and a dog you are familiar with.**

Before interacting with any dog, teach your child how to interact safely with dogs and how to interpret dog behavior to understand what the dog likes and doesn't like. When supervising your child's interactions with dogs, give frequent reminders of what is (and isn't) appropriate behavior. The younger the child, the more closely you need to supervise the interaction. NEVER leave dogs alone with children under age six.

Pay attention to the dog's mood and body language — remember that dogs can feel unwell or grumpy just like children can. Make sure you and your child always approach dogs — even familiar dogs — in a calm and confident manner. This will help the dog feel safe and secure. Always be aware of how the dog responds to the interaction. If the dog is enjoying the interaction, it's fine to continue. Be sure to end the petting or play session before the dog becomes tired, overexcited, or as soon as you notice that the dog has had enough.

Children's personalities vary, and some require closer supervision than others. For example, some children have an easier time following instructions, using good manners, sharing toys, and being respectful of their friends' feelings. Parents and teachers often describe these children as "good listeners." Although these kids should still be supervised when they are interacting with dogs, there is a good chance that they will remember how to treat dogs with respect. Other children tend to be more excitable, less aware of others, and "not such good listeners." These children may require extra supervision because they have a harder time exercising self-control and may not remember the rules for interacting safely with dogs.

3. How to stay safe with dogs you meet indoors.

Keep in mind that when you enter someone's home, you are also entering their dog's home. If you know ahead of time that there is a dog in the house, it's perfectly okay to ask that the dog's owner put the dog on a leash, in its crate, or in another room when you enter.

It is reasonable to expect that when you or your child visit someone, you will not have to endure being knocked over by an excited dog — or bitten by a dog that views you as an intruder. Once you have settled into the visit and you feel comfortable greeting the dog, make sure the dog is on a leash or in a sit-and-stay position before going over to say hello. If you have brought children with you for the visit, make sure you know where the dog is at all times.

4. How to stay safe around dogs outdoors.

Knowing how to interact safely with dogs is empowering for children and helps them overcome their fear of dogs. Teaching children basic safety around dogs includes helping them learn how to understand canine body language and emphasizing that they should always trust their intuition when they're around dogs and other animals. It also includes making sure they know they should never approach an unfamiliar dog outdoors unless the dog is on a leash *and* they have obtained permission from the dog's handler.

Here are two examples of common situations involving dogs outdoors and how children should handle them:

A dog running loose without its owner:

Tell children that if they encounter a dog running loose outside, they should walk calmly indoors (if possible), or else stand very still and tell a grown-up immediately that there is a dog running loose. You (or another responsible adult) should then call animal control — or if you feel safe doing so, you can check to see if the dog has tags and call the owner. If in doubt, stay far away from the dog. If the dog approaches you and/or the child, follow the "be a tree" exercise.

Playing with a familiar dog outdoors:

When children are playing with a familiar dog in a friend's backyard or at the park, remind them to treat the dog gently and to avoid over-exciting it, which might lead to them being knocked over or nipped.

This chapter looked at how important it is to supervise children around dogs and how to stay safe around them. The next chapter will help you understand how dogs communicate and how to read dog body language.

Chapter 7:
How Dogs Communicate

"Dogs do speak, but only to those who know how to listen."

—Orhan Pamuk

"After I wasn't scared of dogs anymore, I became kind of like a detective. I was always trying to figure out what my grandma's dog Barney was trying to say. He talked to me through his body and also his bark. It's pretty cool how dogs talk to us. I learned how to tell when he wanted to be pet and when he wanted to be left alone."

— Kayla, age 11

This chapter will provide a brief overview to help you learn the basics of dog body language and the sounds dogs make to communicate. After *you* have learned some basics, you can help educate your child about how dogs communicate. You can also reinforce the importance of listening to what the dog is telling you and be respectful of the dog's needs.

Teaching kids to pay attention to how dogs communicate will not only help keep them safe but can also enhance their interactions with dogs. When we understand what dogs are telling us, it helps us feel safe, calm, and in control. Dogs show us with their bodies when they want to play and when they prefer to be left alone. Like people, dogs sometimes use their voices to communicate as well. It's important to realize that dogs are individuals, just like people, and different dogs will interact and behave differently depending on their personality, mood, and the situation. The resources section of this book has suggestions on where to find more detailed information on dog communication.

[Author's note: The contributions of humane educator Cathy Malkin are in italics.]

Dogs are excellent communicators who offer clear signals about their feelings and needs — although these signals can seem subtle to human eyes and ears, especially if you're not used to looking for them. In any interaction with dogs, it's important to pay attention to these signals — ignoring them can create a bad situation for both the people and the dog(s).

Understanding how dogs communicate and being able to interpret their body language and vocalizations will tell you when it's okay to interact with a dog and when it's best to stay away. It's important to pay attention to what a dog is communicating, whether it's a dog you've never met before or one you know well.

Children encounter dogs in a variety of situations, and they need to be able to understand how dogs communicate in order to interact with them safely. Understanding dog communication and behavior helps children who are afraid of dogs feel more empowered and comfortable and helps children who enjoy being around dogs feel more connected to them.

*Part of interacting safely with dogs is telling the dogs through your own body language that **you** are safe for them to be around. Dogs feel most comfortable when the people around them move in a calm, deliberate way rather than making quick or jerky movements.*

Seeing things from the dog's point of view

Dogs deserve respect, just like people do. Learning how an interaction looks and feels from the dog's point of view helps children behave in a way that puts the dog and your child at ease.

The first thing to understand about dogs is that they need personal space, just like people do. Sometimes our desire to interact with a dog can make the dog feel very anxious and overwhelmed. When explaining why and how we need to respect a dog's need for space, ask your child to think about how they would feel if someone they didn't know stared at them, got really close to them, or touched them without asking their permission. It would probably make them feel uncomfortable. Many dogs feel the same way when strangers want to pet them.

Dogs express their discomfort through body language. Dogs that feel overwhelmed or threatened may respond by acting aggressively. It is important to pay attention and watch for signs of stress whenever you or your child are interacting with a dog. If the dog's behavior tells you that he may be uncomfortable with being touched or that you are standing too close, back up and give the dog some space.

Dogs use obvious as well as subtle signals to express how they feel. These signals often change quickly, so you need to stay alert and observant when interacting with dogs. Luckily, dogs use specific and consistent behaviors to communicate their feelings, so it's easy to tell what a dog is saying as long as you know what to look for. Understanding a dog's body language will let you know when it's safe and appropriate for your child to interact with the dog, whether it's the family dog or a friend's dog.

Understanding dog body language

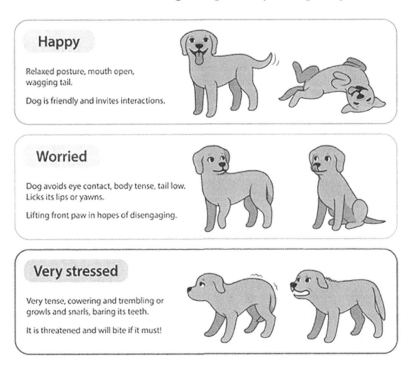

Happy

Relaxed posture, mouth open, wagging tail.

Dog is friendly and invites interactions.

Worried

Dog avoids eye contact, body tense, tail low. Licks its lips or yawns.

Lifting front paw in hopes of disengaging.

Very stressed

Very tense, cowering and trembling or growls and snarls, baring its teeth.

It is threatened and will bite if it must!

The above chart gives some basic dog body language examples. Please refer to the back of the book for additional resources.

Dog Stress Signals

When a dog is feeling stressed, you will notice that their behavior looks out of context from their typical behavior. Below are the most common signals of stress, according to Doggonesafe.com:

- ❑ The dog moves away from the child.
- ❑ The dog doesn't look at the child or turns his head away from the child.
- ❑ The dog looks at you with a pleading expression, "Please help me. I'm feeling stressed out and I want you to make this feeling and pressure stop."
- ❑ You can see the "whites" of the dog's eyes in a half-moon shape, indicating stress and fear.
- ❑ The dog yawns while the child approaches or is interacting with him.
- ❑ The dog licks his chops or flicks his tongue over his nose while the child approaches or is interacting with him.
- ❑ The dog suddenly starts scratching, biting, or licking himself.
- ❑ The dog "checks out" and starts sniffing odd objects like the ground or a wall.
- ❑ The dog does a big "wet-dog shake" after the child stops touching him.

©Doggone Safe

If you are with a dog that is exhibiting any of these stress signals, it is best to slowly back away from the dog. Be careful not to stare directly into the dog's eyes. In dog language, staring into their eyes is a threat and can be an invitation to act aggressively. Backing up and disengaging takes the pressure off the dog and allows him to relax. Once the dog doesn't perceive you as a threat, you can gently invite them to interact with you. However, be respectful and accept that not all dogs want to interact.

Dave and Gina's Story

When Dave and Gina adopted their new dog, Molly, the thought of having children was still in the distant future. The rescue organization warned the couple that Molly might not be good with infants and children. While Gina intuitively knew there was a potential for Molly to bite, she put it out of her mind until they had their first child.

When they brought Oscar home from the hospital, they placed him and Molly on the bed together. Molly showed stress signals with her ears pinned back and yawning. Not understanding that Molly was saying she was uncomfortable, they initiated an interaction between Molly and the baby by putting Oscar's feet near the dog. Molly immediately expressed her fear by licking her lips. Not aware of what their dog was communicating, Dave took Molly's paw and placed it on top of Oscar. Molly immediately turned and snarled at Dave — a strong signal that she was not comfortable and wanted the interaction to stop at once. At that point, Dave immediately took Molly off the bed, which prevented the situation from getting worse. It was a difficult decision but they ultimately decided to find a new home for Molly.

Dog Warning Signals

Always be on the lookout for signs of stress in a dog when it is near or interacting with a child. As we learned in Chapter Six, dogs always exhibit warning signs or stress signals before they bite.

A dog that feels threatened is likely to respond in one of three ways:

1. *The dog will freeze.*
2. *The dog will try to get away.*
3. *The dog will stand its ground and attack.*

> Humans experience a similar fight-or-flight response to threatening situations. Children who are afraid of dogs may run away from them, feel paralyzed from fear, and/or scream or cry. Both dogs and children want to feel some level of control over their environment and they react in similar ways when they feel frightened.

As the adult, it's your responsibility to intervene immediately if you notice any warning signs. Make sure your children stop what they're doing and give the dog space. In many cases, a dog will try to leave the area or turn its back to a child if he is feeling anxious or stressed by a child's behavior. It's important to always provide a way out for the dog; never allow your child to "corner" a dog. Some dogs will hide under a table or seek refuge in their crate if they can. This is a healthy response to stress. But not all dogs respond to stress by simply removing themselves from the situation, so please remain vigilant.

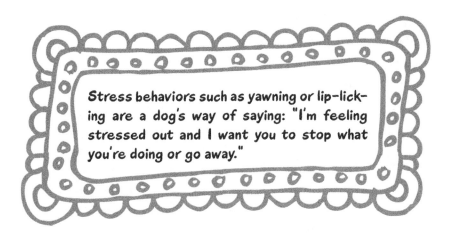

Stress behaviors such as yawning or lip-licking are a dog's way of saying: "I'm feeling stressed out and I want you to stop what you're doing or go away."

Fozzie always greets my grandchildren enthusiastically by wagging his tail and barking "hello." He enjoys being petted and given treats for the first 15 minutes of any visit. Then he goes to lie down on his bed, which is located in the same room where the kids play. The kids will often go over to pet him or show him toys throughout their visit. Sometimes Fozzie will show us he's had enough interaction by leaving the room and going into the kitchen to lie down by the back door instead. When he does this, I explain to the children that Fozzie doesn't want to play right now and we need to give him some privacy. Inevitably, the child/dog interactions begin again during snack time, when the kids share their Goldfish crackers with Fozzie.

Unlike human behavior, dog behavior and body language are consistent and predictable. Aggressive behavior such as biting rarely comes without warning because dogs communicate their feelings through body language and vocalizations. Learning to interpret their communication is an essential part of interacting with dogs safely and allows you to intervene before a dog's discomfort escalates to aggression.

It may be helpful to think about "reading" dog behavior in terms of traffic light colors: green (all is well; it's fine to proceed), yellow (caution — pull back and give the dog some space), red (stop what you're doing immediately). Whenever you or your child are interacting with a dog, keep an eye out for signals that the dog is feeling uncomfortable, stressed, or scared. If at any time you see the dog exhibiting any of the behaviors

listed in the yellow or red warning signs, stop the interaction immediately and separate the child from the dog.

Green Light

It's okay to approach and interact with the dog, as long as you have permission from the dog's handler.

- ❑ *The dog is leashed and is under the handler's control.*
- ❑ *The dog's body language is relaxed, calm, and welcoming.*
- ❑ *The dog sits before you approach and stays seated (or standing calmly) during the interaction.*

If you meet an unfamiliar dog, only approach the dog if the handler gives permission.

Look for relaxed and calm canine body language before allowing a child to play with any dog.

Yellow Light — Warning Signals

Immediately intervene and stop the interaction if the dog is exhibiting any of the following signs of stress.

When a dog displays these signals, it's their way of saying, "I'm uncomfortable and I don't like what's going on. I need you to make it stop right now."

1. *The dog starts yawning but isn't tired.*
2. *The dog is licking its lips, but there is no food around.*
3. *The dog rolls its eyes so that the whites are visible at the edges.*
4. *The dog turns its back to the child (or adult).*
5. *The dog behaves in an excited manner such as lunging or jumping up.*
6. *The handler does not have the dog under control.*

Look out for avoidant behaviors:

Never let your child follow or try to interact with a dog that is moving away from them. Always allow dogs to decide whether they want to interact with you or your child. If a dog chooses to move away, respect the dog's wishes. If you are interacting with a dog and it decides to move away, understand that this means the dog is feeling stressed or uncomfortable and is choosing to remove itself from the situation. The dog is making a good decision, and it's important for both the dog's comfort and your safety to respect that decision and leave the dog alone.

Teach children to respect dogs' feelings and their decisions and make sure they stop interacting with any dog that is showing signs of stress or moving away from them. Ignoring these signals can lead to aggressive behavior such as biting, especially if the dog feels cornered or trapped by the child.

Red Light — Immediate Danger

The dog is about to bite. Separate the child from the dog immediately.

These behaviors are strong warnings that the dog is about to act aggressively. If you see a dog do any of the following, you must immediately remove your child from the dog's presence:

- ❑ *The dog's body stiffens or freezes.*
- ❑ *The dog stops panting and holds its breath.*
- ❑ *The dog lifts its upper lip.*
- ❑ *The dog growls or snarls.*

It's also essential to <u>listen</u> for warning signals: **Dogs** rarely growl without good cause, and growling is their final warning signal before biting.

If you fail to respond to a dog's early warning signals, it will most likely begin vocalizing its distress. Growling or snarling are signs that the dog's stress has escalated to a breaking point and it is preparing to bite. Immediately remove your child from the situation.

Dogs also use their voices to communicate in a variety of ways.

The following excerpt from the American Society for Prevention of Cruelty to Animals (ASPCA) describes the most common reasons for barking[15]:

- ❑ **Territorial Barking**
- ❑ **Alarm Barking**
- ❑ **Attention-Seeking Barking**
- ❑ **Greeting Barking**
- ❑ **Compulsive Barking**
- ❑ **Socially Facilitated Barking**
- ❑ **Frustration-Induced Barking**

Some dogs also tend to be more vocal than others because of their breed or individual personalities. Fozzie's breed, the Keeshond, is known to be very vocal. They were originally bred in the Netherlands to be companion dogs on barges. Their job was to alert the captain of anything out of the ordinary. Fozzie barks for many reasons. Among these are: to alert us that someone is walking down the street, to let us know he is happy to see us when we come home, and to tell us he wants attention.

How Dogs Communicate That They Want to Interact

Through their body language, dogs tell us when they're feeling content, when they want to express affection, and when they want to play. The "translations" of dog body language below should be considered guidelines rather than definitive rules. When interpreting a dog's behavior, please remember to take into account what you know about the dog's personality as well as the specific situation.

Watch the tail

A dog's tail may wag to say hello or to tell us that the dog is friendly and would like to be petted. Of course, different dogs have different kinds of tails. Fozzie's tail sits up on his back in a curlicue. When he wags it, his whole back end wiggles. Retrievers have big tails that swish back and forth when they are happy (I have seen an exuberant tail knock a few things off a table now and then). However, remember that not all tail movements indicate that a dog is feeling friendly — a stiff, slow-moving tail is a warning sign.

Watch the face

Dog trainer Annie Phenix says, "Dogs show affection with their faces. What's happening with a dog's face when she is happy with a human? Dogs can smile or grin. In general, you want to see an open, relaxed mouth and not a shut-tight grimace. Panting can be a sign of stress, so a happy dog might have her mouth open toward you, but [she] shouldn't be excessively panting — unless it's a hot day or she has been exercising. Canine language must be taken in context."

Watch the eyes

According to Phenix, "The 'I-love-you' dog eyes are not hard but soft, round, and probably looking you right in the eyes, which is completely different than a hard stare with little to no blinking coming from a dog — that's a warning to back up. You also don't want to approach a dog showing 'whale eyes,' where the eyes are wide, and you can see the whites around the pupils."[16]

Dogs also like to play and interact with other dogs. According to the American Kennel Club (AKC), the following behaviors often indicate that a dog wants to play with another dog:

Behaviors that say dogs are just being playful

1. The play bow — front end down, back end in the air. Sometimes the dog trying to initiate play will slap his front legs down on the ground repeatedly.
2. A big, silly, open-mouthed grin.
3. Exaggerated, bouncy movements.
4. Loud, continuous growling and snarling that sounds exaggerated. Play-growling may sound scarier than serious fighting.
5. Dogs voluntarily making themselves vulnerable by "falling" down and exposing their bellies and/or allowing themselves to be caught when chasing one another. Dogs often take turns chasing one another when playing.
6. Dogs that keep going back for more. Even the dog that ends up on his back doesn't want to stop playing. Dogs who are playing happily will probably take turns acting out play-fighting behaviors.

On the other hand, a dog that exhibits the following behaviors is saying they do ***not*** want to play:

Behaviors that tell you this is not a game

1. The dogs' bodies get very stiff. Hackles (the hair on a dog's upper back) are raised. You may not be able to see this if the dog has long hair.
2. Closed mouth, curled lip, low warning growl.
3. Movements will be quick and efficient — no bouncing around, no taking turns.
4. Ears will be pinned flat and lips curled back — there may be snarling. No big silly smiles.
5. If the dogs get into actual combat, hopefully it will be a short encounter, and the "loser" will try to leave the area.
6. One dog may be trying to get away from the other dog(s), with body language that is *not* happy and bouncy (e.g., tail tucked down).[17]

Signs that a Dog is Receptive to Attention or Wants to Play

According to Doggonesafe[18], a dog-bite prevention education organization, signs of a happy dog include:

- ❑ Loose, wiggly body.
- ❑ Relaxed, soft facial expression.
- ❑ Lying with one paw tucked under the other.
- ❑ Enthusiastic tail wagging with a wiggly rear end.
- ❑ Play bow (front end down, rear end up, wagging tail)

Here is how an interaction with new people might look and feel from a dog's point of view:

You (the dog) are walking down the street on a leash with your person. It has just rained and there are many interesting smells. You notice an adult and a young child walking toward you. You like meeting new people, so your body and mouth soften at the thought of saying hello to them. As the people get closer, you wag your tail in greeting. Your person says "hello" to the new people and glances down at you to make sure you are behaving politely and to see if you are interested in saying hello to them, too. You let your person know that you would like to say hello by lifting your ears, wagging your tail and hindquarters enthusiastically, and moving toward the new people.

Your person then asks you to sit. You quickly obey, as you're hoping to get a treat for being a good dog as well as looking forward to saying hello to the people. Your person stays calm and relaxed because they know you're calm around small children and like being with them. You feel safe knowing that your person is in control of the situation. The adult reminds the child to ask your person if it's ok to pet you.

How to Teach Children about Dog Communication

Now that you understand how dogs communicate and can read their body language, you can teach your children to do the same. It's easiest for children to learn new things in small doses over time. Think about how children learn the alphabet or how to swim.

Hopefully, nature and animals are an integral part of your child's life. This way there will be plenty of opportunities to teach them about dog communication. It's best to try a few different methods and remember that it may take a while for the child to learn to "speak dog."

For example, if you and the child are reading a story that includes pictures of dogs, discuss the dog's body language and "quiz" the child to see if they can interpret the dog's body language accurately. You can also do this using videos or photos. After your child has completed the OFOD Protocol exposure therapy, try going back to the photos and videos that you used during the therapy to see if your child has a better understanding of how dogs communicate after having interacted with a real dog. When you greet a neighbor's dog or see a dog through the window, ask your child to tell you what they notice about the dog and what the dog is showing them with their body. It's important to notice how a dog communicates with its whole body — not just its tail or ears.

Nine-year-old Chelsea told me that she lives in a neighborhood with lots of dogs and she often sees them walk by her house with their people. After working with Fozzie and me, she said she and her mother play a game where they sit and watch dogs out the living room bay window. Chelsea told me about some of the dogs they watch. She said she can tell that Jo-Jo, a small brown and white dog, was afraid of the bigger dogs. Chelsea said she knew this because every time a large dog approached, Jo-Jo would crouch down and put her tail between her legs until the bigger dog passed by. Chelsea also said she can tell that Jo-Jo likes people because when a person without a dog approaches, Jo-Jo comes right up to them. She added that Jo-Jo walks with an easy gait and has a relaxed facial expression, as if hoping for a treat. Chelsea noted that the friendliest and happiest dog in her whole neighborhood is Lily, a big Bernese Mountain Dog. Chelsea said she can tell that Lily is happy and feels at ease because she has a bounce in her step and her eyes, ears, and mouth look relaxed. Whenever Lily comes across a person or another dog, her body stays relaxed, and she pricks her ears forward and wags her tail.

For more teaching tools about dog communication, visit the Resource Section of this book.

When to Approach/Not Approach a Dog

- ❑ **The best time to approach a dog is when it is sitting in response to a "sit" command.** Not only is a dog who is sitting calmly less likely to jump up on a child, but seeing a dog obey a command (whether their own or the handler's) also gives children a sense of control.

- ❑ **Never approach an overly excited dog.** If the dog is jumping up or lunging at you, it is better to wait until the dog calms down before approaching.

- ❑ **Never approach a dog that has its back turned.** Dogs often turn away from people when they are feeling stressed and want to avoid contact. You also do not want to surprise an unsuspecting dog by touching it.

- ❑ **Do not approach when a dog holds its tail stiffly or seems tense.**

- ❑ **If a dog suddenly freezes (stops moving), do *not* approach.** This is a strong warning sign.

In this chapter, we learned how dogs communicate so we can interpret their body language and vocalizations. Being able to understand dogs' signals not only helps us stay safe around dogs, it can also help us have more rewarding interactions with them. When playing with their human friends, children have to learn to share, take turns, and communicate their needs. It's no different with dogs. Understanding that dogs have many of the same needs as children and knowing how they communicate helps children interact safely with dogs and makes it more fun to spend time with them.

Chapter 8:
How Children Can Benefit from Relationships with Dogs

"Until one has loved an animal, a part of one's soul remains unawakened."
— Anatole France

"When I was sick in bed for two weeks with mono(nucleosis), I remember that Mugsy never left my side. He helped me feel less lonely, and I had someone to talk to."

— Becky, age 12

In this chapter, we will look at how all the hard work you've done with your child to help them feel safe and comfortable around dogs pays off. Interactions and relationships with canines can greatly enhance our lives. Although we are focusing on dogs, many of the same benefits can be gained from developing relationships with other companion animals.

> **Animals can enrich the lives of children in many ways — from strengthening their sense of compassion and empathy to helping them learn responsibility and a reverence for nature.**

Overcoming fear and learning how to safely interact with dogs will also make your child feel more confident and empowered. Knowing that they can be brave even when they are afraid is a life skill that can translate into other situations. Some of these examples include diving into a pool for the first time, doing a presentation in class, or telling a friend when they are being unkind. Going through the process described in this book can also help children feel more comfortable speaking up for themselves.

I know the many benefits of spending time with dogs and other animals from personal experience. When I take Fozzie for a walk after a long day, I begin to feel less stressed as soon as we step out the door. Watching Fozzie as he looks for squirrels and yummy things to smell helps me become aware of my surroundings and more rooted in the moment. Dogs live in the present, and spending time with them helps us remember to pay attention to the sights, sounds, and other sensations around us. This mindfulness can help us manage daily stress and reduce anxiety.

It has been my personal mission to share my love of dogs with others. My children's lives have been enhanced by their interactions with our dogs and guinea pigs. Some of the things they've learned from these relationships include developing a reverence for nature, learning to consider the feelings of others, developing a sense of responsibility (such as making sure the dog has water in his bowl), knowing how and when to put their own needs after those of the animal, and learning to find a respite from the demands of everyday life by taking a calm moment to stroke the animal's fur. Now that my children are grown, we are all helping *their* children learn these same things. My heart comes close to bursting when the entire family, including Fozzie, is in our living room spending time together.

Most children have a natural affinity for animals. They experience the animal kingdom from an early age through nursery rhymes, picture books, cartoons, and video games that feature animals as characters. Many of a baby's first words are the names of animals and the sounds they make. They learn to identify animals in pictures and to respond when their parents ask, "What does a cow say?"

If your child enjoys stuffed animals, consider giving them realistic-looking stuffed dogs so they can practice taking care of an animal. You can provide small feeding dishes, grooming tools to "care for" their plush pup, and even a veterinarian's kit.

The Family Dog

Many families treat their dogs as members of the family. The dog is included in the family portrait on holiday cards, and many families celebrate the dog's birthday or the day the dog joined the family (known as the "gotcha" day). Dogs often accompany their families on vacation, and when that isn't practical, they are boarded at carefully chosen dog "resorts." The family dog's needs are considered just as carefully as those of other family members. My son once commented that I spent more time finding places to board our dog than I did looking for summer camps for him. To this day, we rent a beach house for a week in the summer so Fozzie can swim.

Growing up, my sister and I both experienced the benefits of developing close relationships with dogs. These experiences had such an impact on us that we both became humane educators. Our goal is to teach children to treat **all** living things with kindness and respect. The mission of humane education is to help people develop empathy and compassion for other people and for animals, respect for the environment, and the ability to make decisions based on the welfare of others as well as themselves.

> "So many of our values, beliefs, and biases are developed at a young age. Humane education nurtures compassion and respect for all beings and teaches children to see non-human animals as individuals with emotions, intelligence, and their own interests, and as deserving of equal consideration… When we are raised from infancy to care about the needs and interests of everyone, then our life choices cultivate a kinder, more just world for all."[19]

As parents, you have many opportunities to help your children learn to love and respect animals. Some of these include going to nature centers and learning about the animals that are native to your community. You can reinforce respect for the environment by reminding your children that it is important not to litter and not to release balloons into the sky because this can harm wildlife. When a storybook includes animals, discuss how the animals feel. In my house, we stopped going to the circus and I explained that I did not want to support animals being used that way. If you have access to live animals, such as grandma's cat, help your child recognize and respect how the cat is feeling.

Benefits of the Human-Animal Bond

Dogs leave huge paw prints on the lives they touch.

There is no doubt that our lives are enriched by the presence of animals. If we pay attention, we can learn a lot from dogs. Over the last decade or so, many reputable organizations have done studies on the benefits of being around dogs. I don't need a study to tell me that a classroom of six-year-olds immediately comes to life when you walk in with a dog. Or when Fozzie rolls over to ask for a belly rub, I feel love for him and very peaceful in that moment. I also feel honored that he trusts me enough to be so vulnerable. My heart swells when he gently sniffs my grandchildren's ears or gives them a nose kiss and they squeal with delight. My two-year-old grandson barely says hello to me when he comes to visit. His first question is "Where's Fozzie?" My baby granddaughter's first words were "woof woof."

Interacting with dogs can have many positive effects on people. In addition to their number-one role of providing us with acceptance and unconditional love, some dogs also perform important jobs that require specific training as well as relying on the special relationship between dogs and humans.

Fozzie is a **therapy dog**, which means that in addition to having a calm, gentle temperament, he has been specially trained to provide emotional support and comfort to people in hospitals, schools, and other places. As a therapy dog, Fozzie has helped many people. He has encouraged older people to reminisce about their childhood memories involving dogs. Children have read to him and told him their secrets, such as feeling jealous of their siblings. When Fozzie and I visit schools as a team, we teach kids how to interact safely with dogs and how to treat all animals with kindness. Fozzie loves doing this work, and it is one of my favorite things to do as well.

There are also **service dogs** who go through rigorous, specialized training so they can help people with physical or emotional disabilities. Seeing-eye dogs are probably the most well-known service dogs, but dogs can also be trained to help children who have autism and veterans with PTSD. Other dogs are trained to sense seizures or low blood sugar. These dogs alert their person so they can make sure they're in a safe place/position before a seizure or adjust their insulin.

Emotional support or **comfort dogs** are a more recently developed service category. All dogs provide their humans with comfort and companionship. For people with mental illnesses or other emotional disabilities, mental health professionals can provide documentation that allows the patient to register their dog as an emotional support dog. This allows the dog to accompany the person into places where dogs wouldn't usually be allowed.

Fozzie says: It's important to reserve the emotional-support service animal credential for people who have a medically verified need.

Four Benefits of Spending Time with Dogs

Interacting with dogs can enrich our lives in many ways. For children, the benefits of spending time with dogs include:

1. **Emotional benefits**
2. **Development of positive character traits**
3. **Social skills**
4. **Physical and health benefits**

EMOTIONAL BENEFITS

- ☐ **Love**
- ☐ **Empathy**
- ☐ **Self-confidence and pride**
- ☐ **Anxiety/stress reduction**

Interacting with dogs on a regular basis has a wide range of emotional benefits for children. After working through the process in this book, your child is hopefully feeling more comfortable around dogs and may even be ready to begin enjoying some of these benefits.

Love

Dogs give us unconditional love, regardless of what's going on in our lives. Animals don't make judgments. There aren't any negative consequences of telling a dog your secrets or wishes. They don't care if you have the newest gadgets or fancy clothes; they are just happy to be with you. They ask very little from us. Food, water, shelter, love, medical care, and attention are all they need to be happy and healthy. Humans are hardwired to love, and dogs make wonderful partners. Our dogs trust us to take care of them, and in caring for a dog we develop special bonds with them.

Loving and trusting relationships are vital to the emotional health and well-being of children. Children's first and most important bond is, of course, with their parents. Developing a close relationship with the family dog is another opportunity for children to experience and express love. Dogs provide an opportunity for children to see the world from another creature's viewpoint and to learn empathy — the ability to understand how someone else feels.

Empathy

Playing with dogs or watching puppies frolic together can lighten our spirits and make us feel happy. Dogs can help us feel calm when we pet them. They can help us feel needed when we feed or brush them. We also feel sad when a dog we love is sick or hurt. Even though these are difficult emotions to experience, we feel them because we are empathizing with the dog. When a dog is very ill or elderly, we worry about their health and we grieve when our beloved pets die. For many children, the death of a pet is their first experience of loss, and the sudden absence of their daily companion leaves a void.

Keisha's Story, Age Ten

I met ten-year-old Keisha at a Kindness to Animals program I led during her school's health fair. She shared with the group that her dog Milo had been at the vet for several days due to vomiting and dehydration. She said she felt scared and worried that he might die. She also felt very sad that he must feel scared and alone because he was so sick and not at home with his family. She begged her mother to get permission to visit him at the animal hospital, and she brought him her special teddy bear, which she knew would cheer him up. Keisha's story shows her strong connection with Milo and her concern and empathy for how he was feeling.

Self-Confidence and Pride

Interacting with dogs can help boost children's self-confidence and sense of pride in their accomplishments. For example, when a child asks a dog to sit and the dog follows the command, the child feels competent and proud. When a dog greets a child with a wagging tail and happy demeanor, the child feels special and important. They also offer us unfailing friendship, unconditional love, and non-critical companionship.

When I was in seventh grade, my pet dogs and guinea pigs got me through a very rough patch. When I felt that none of the other kids at school liked me, there was always someone who was happy to see me and keep me company when I got home. Freida, our Yorkshire terrier, kept me company while I read in bed, and General Mustard, my guinea pig, sat on my lap while I watched *The Brady Bunch* and petted him.

Anxiety/Stress Reduction

Pets' unconditional acceptance of us helps us feel valued for who we are and can reduce anxiety. The simple act of stroking a pet's fur fulfills the basic human need for touch, and children often find it especially enjoyable. For both children and adults, spending time with dogs helps calm and center us in the present so we can pay attention to what we're doing now instead of worrying about tomorrow's math test or whether we'll be invited to a party. These moments provide welcome breaks from our challenging world.

Many people also feel safer having a dog at home. I feel more secure knowing that I have a "watchdog" who will alert us not only when the FedEx truck arrives or if there are pesky squirrels outside, but also if someone tries to break into the house.

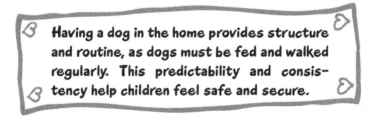

Having a dog in the home provides structure and routine, as dogs must be fed and walked regularly. This predictability and consistency help children feel safe and secure.

DEVELOPMENT OF POSITIVE CHARACTER TRAITS

- ❑ **Kindness**
- ❑ **Respect**
- ❑ **Responsibility**

"Children learn what they live." — Dorothy Law Nolte

Learning values such as kindness and respect for other living things is an important part of growing up because these principles help determine how we live our lives and how we treat others. Kids are like sponges; they soak up everything they see around them. They learn not just from what we tell them, but also by watching us and imitating what we do. When a child sees their parent or guardian get out of bed early in the morning because the dog needs to go out, the child learns that the needs of other creatures are important.

Kindness

Interacting with animals helps children learn to treat others with kindness. When adults interact appropriately with dogs and take care of their needs, we are modeling how to treat animals with kindness and respect. When you teach children to be kind to animals, you are also teaching them to be kind to their friends and to other people. When children see us slow the car down for a squirrel running across the street or allow someone with only one item to check out ahead of us at the supermarket, we are modeling kindness. For example, my own children learned early on that whenever we made plans, we always needed to take the dog's needs into account. How long would we be out? Would we be home to give him dinner? Did we need to call a dog walker?

One of my favorite stories about learning to be kind is this Cherokee Folk Tale:

An old Cherokee was teaching his grandson about life. "A fight is going on inside me," he said to the boy. "It is a terrible fight, and it is between two wolves. One is evil — he is anger, envy, sorrow, regret, greed, arrogance, self-pity, guilt, resentment, inferiority, lies, false pride, superiority, and ego."

He continued, "The other is good — he is joy, peace, love, hope, serenity, humility, kindness, benevolence, empathy, generosity, truth, compassion, and faith. The same fight is going on inside you — and inside every other person, too."

The grandson thought about it for a minute and then asked his grandfather, "Which wolf will win?"

The old Cherokee simply replied, "The one you feed."
Source: https://urbanbalance.com/the-story-of-two-wolves

Respect

Animals also help us teach our children to respect the feelings of others. One of the things kids learn from helping to care for a family pet is that animals have feelings, too. When we teach kids to consider and respect the feelings of a dog, it helps them learn to consider the feelings of their friends and family as well. It is also

185

important to teach children to respect and help protect wildlife and the environment.

In my humane education programs, I teach children to think about the effect their behavior will have on animals and their habitats. For example, the plastic rings that hold together a six-pack of soda should be cut up before being discarded because small animals can get their heads stuck in them. I often start these discussions by talking about balloons. While balloons are fun and pretty, they are devastating to wildlife. Birds can get caught in the strings and other animals may die from eating the deflated balloons. When parents teach their children about protecting the environment and model responsible behavior toward wildlife, we all benefit. Respect and caring are contagious.

Responsibility

Dogs can help children develop caregiving skills and a sense of responsibility. Kids can begin learning how to nurture others by helping to care for dogs. This plants the seeds for responsibility and helps children learn to consider the needs of others. It feels good to help others, especially those who cannot help themselves, like our pets. I explain to the kids I work with that dogs (and other pets) are like babies who never grow up. Children will grow up and eventually be able to drive or use public transportation, make meals for themselves, have jobs, and take care of themselves. But our pets depend on us to take care of them, and when we bring dogs or other pets into our homes, we must understand that we are making a commitment to take care of them for their whole lives. Adopting an animal means taking on the responsibility of caring for another living thing. Having that experience helps children understand the importance of responsibility and commitment.

SOCIAL SKILLS

- ❑ **Patience and Self-Control**
- ❑ **Boundaries**

❑ Communication Skills

Developing social skills is also an important part of growing up and learning to take care of oneself. Good social skills do not guarantee a happy life, but they certainly help us develop healthy and satisfying relationships, do well in school, and get along with others at work and in other social situations. Using good manners, respecting personal space, having self-control, being a good communicator, and learning to share provide good foundations for all interactions.

Patience and Self-Control

Patience is an important social skill. Children need to learn to wait their turn to ask or answer questions in school and to wait patiently for their turn to throw or kick the ball when playing sports. Children who learn self-control have been shown to enjoy greater success in a variety of ways later in life than those who have trouble developing self-control.

Self-control is part of learning to interact and play with dogs safely. As we saw in Chapter Six, kids must learn to pause and "read" a dog's behavior to determine if it's okay to pet the dog, rather than running up to the dog and immediately interacting with it. Children who grow up with dogs also learn to wait their turn while the dog is getting a meal, water, or snacks. Dogs also have to learn patience and self-control as part of their training, and I like to point out to children that Fozzie will wait patiently for me to put his leash and collar on before we go for a walk.

Boundaries

Another social skill children have to learn is how to respect personal space — most children don't have an inherent sense of when they are standing too close to someone when they're waiting in line or having a conversation. Just as we don't want a dog to invade our personal space by jumping on us, we should respect dogs when they let us know we are getting too close to them and they are uncomfortable.

Dogs provide immediate feedback when a child is tugging its fur too tightly or using too loud a voice. James, a 13-year-old boy I worked with, had difficulty controlling his emotions. When he interacted with Mugsy, my first Keeshond, James was able to see Mugsy's physical reactions, which gave him clear information about how Mugsy was feeling. When James spoke in a loud and angry voice while standing very close to Mugsy, Mugsy pinned his ears back, began to pant, and looked to me for reassurance. I then asked James to take some deep breaths, soften his voice, and step back a foot or two. Mugsy immediately became more comfortable and relaxed. James was able to see the impact of his behavior. This helped him understand that his actions affected others.

Eleven-year-old Jonah told me a similar story about his dog, Stella. He noticed that whenever he and his father were arguing about chores in loud voices, Stella would become nervous and leave the room. But if they spoke in their everyday tone of voice, she stayed calm and remained in the room with them.

Communication Skills

Dogs are wonderful ice breakers and conversation starters. It's easy to ask questions about someone's dog or to tell someone about your dog. I've noticed that at many social functions, we end up talking about our dogs. For some reason, it seems more socially acceptable to "brag" or tell stories about your dog than it is to brag about your children's accomplishments. Dogs and other animals are also topics that most kids like to talk about. I work with a number of children who have social anxiety and are often hesitant to engage in conversation, but when there is a dog involved, they are almost always more willing to talk.

When I am out walking Fozzie, groups of children will often run up to us wanting to pet him. After I explain to the kids that they need to take turns petting him, I almost always see a lot of animated conversation about him. They say "Oh, he's so cute!" or ask, "How old is he?" and "What's his name?" Encountering a dog sparks interaction with one another as well as with the dog and its handler.

PHYSICAL AND HEALTH BENEFITS

- ❑ **Sensory Experiences**
- ❑ **Exercise**
- ❑ **Relaxation**

Sensory Experiences

As soon as they're born, children begin learning about their world through their senses. They hear their parents' voices, they smell and taste milk or formula, they see adoring smiles, and they feel gentle caresses. As they grow, they continue to use their senses to experience and make sense of the world. Dogs provide a wide range of sensory experiences. Their fur is soft to the touch. They may smell "doggy" fresh from a bath. It's fun to watch them play. Their barks and other vocalizations help us stay aware of our surroundings. When Fozzie barks, I immediately stop what I'm doing and pay attention to whatever might be going on.

Exercise

Families with dogs are often very active. Many families take their dogs camping or boating. Dog walking is an excellent form of exercise. Every day, no matter the weather, Fozzie and I go for a 20- to 30-minute walk. This is good for my body and also for my mental health. I usually feel less overwhelmed and stressed about my daily life after a walk. Throwing balls and running around the backyard are also excellent ways for children and dogs to get exercise.

Health Benefits

Being with a dog has health benefits for people of all ages:

- ❑ Pet owners are less likely to suffer from depression than those without pets.
- ❑ People with pets have lower blood pressure in stressful situations than those without pets. One study even found that when people with borderline hypertension adopted dogs from a shelter, their blood pressure declined significantly within five months.
- ❑ Pet owners have lower triglyceride and cholesterol levels (indicators of heart disease) than those without pets.
- ❑ Heart attack patients with pets survive longer than those without.
- ❑ Pet owners over age 65 make 30 percent fewer visits to their doctors than those without pets.
- ❑ While people with pets often experience the greatest health benefits, a pet doesn't necessarily have to be a dog or a cat. Even watching fish in an aquarium can help reduce muscle tension and lower pulse rate.[20]

Kristen's Story, Age Eight

Kristen's personal experience with her family dog perfectly sums up the benefits of spending time with dogs. I asked eight-year-old Kristen what it's like to have a dog and whether she has learned anything from being a "sister" to a furry friend. This is what she told me about her Golden Retriever, Luna, who was five years old at the time.

"Well, we got Luna as a puppy when I was still a little kid (age three). I remember running all over the house with her and falling down, and she would climb on me and kiss me a lot. My brother, who is two years older than me, was kind of rough with Luna, so my mom yelled at him to be gentle. Luna never bit or even growled at us, but sometimes she would put herself in her crate — kind of like a time-out. But I think she was just tired of playing with us. I love Luna, and she is my best friend. One day I had a fight with my friend, and I was crying on my bed. Luna came running and licked my tears away. When I pet her or throw a ball to her, I smile a lot. It's my job to make sure she has fresh water every day, and one day I forgot to fill the bowl. I felt so bad that I had made her feel thirsty. I hope Luna lives forever."

Relaxation

Playing with a dog increases levels of serotonin and dopamine, which can help you feel calm and relaxed. When you sit and lay with a calm dog, both of you are in a space of relaxation. Petting a dog helps you be in the moment and shifts your state into relaxation because it releases feel-good hormones such as endorphins and oxytocin. Your breathing slows down and becomes deeper and your heart rate is slowing down too, which gives the nervous system a nice break. In addition, the feel of the soft fur can also be very soothing; the repetitive movement of stroking is a very calming sensation and can even feel like a meditation.

Fozzie says: While dogs can enrich the lives of children, they may not be the right choice for every family. The adults in the home must make sure that their animal's needs are met — including food, water, exercise, medical care, and attention/affection. DO NOT expect any child under the age of 18 to take responsibility for the family dog or for any animal.

While dogs are my favorite pet, if it's not practical for your family to have one, you may want to consider another type of animal companion such as fish, a bird, a cat, or a guinea pig. In many ways, these pets can provide similar experiences and they may require less work to keep them safe and healthy. If an animal companion is not feasible for your family, do not despair. There are many other ways to help your children learn compassion and respect for animals and the environment. You can offer to walk a neighbor's dog, buy special treats/toys for grandma's cat, or collect old linens for the animals at the shelter. Libraries and schools often host visits from therapy dogs and other animals. You can visit nature centers and petting zoos as well. Simple acts like picking up litter and disposing of it responsibly help to keep the habitat of all animals safe.

By now I am sure you can tell how passionate I am about the bond between people and dogs or other companion animals. This special relationship, based on mutual respect and trust, can have a great influence on the well-being of both people and animals, bringing many benefits and adding a lot of fun and comfort to everyday life. Fear — including the fear of dogs — can limit a child's experience and make the world feel smaller. But when a child overcomes their fear of dogs, a whole new world of opportunities and possibilities opens up.

Helpful Forms

Please refer to **Stefanicohen.com** for more information on resources and to download the Questionnaire, Session Logs, and Bravery Certificates. I have provided templates here for you to photocopy as well.

QUESTIONNAIRE

Note: Whenever possible your child should actively participate in answering these questions.

1. At what age did your child's fear of dogs begin and/or when did you first notice it? _____
_____

2. Did your child have a specific negative experience with a dog? If yes, get as much information about the experience as possible. _____
_____

3. Did your child see an incident involving a dog happen to someone else? If yes, get as much information about the experience as possible. _____
_____

4. Did your child hear about an incident involving a dog happen to someone else? If yes, get as much information about

the experience as possible. _____

_____

5. Does your child observe you or another trusted adult being nervous around dogs? If so, whom and how? _____

_____

6. Did your child develop a strong fear of dogs without an obvious triggering event or cause? _____

7. Does your child have other fears? If so, what are they? ____

_____

8. Would you characterize your child as being anxious in general?

_____

9. How motivated is your child to overcome their fear of dogs? Very, somewhat or not really? _____

10. Would you classify your child's fear of dogs as mild, moderate or severe? _____

11. How would you describe your child's personality? Outgoing, reserved, slow to warm up or withdrawn? _____

_____

12. Does your child ask a lot of questions? Do they have a vivid imagination? _____

_____

13. Is your child highly observant and/or extra cautious? ____

_____

Brave with Dogs!

Session Log

Date of Session	
Participants	
Session Duration	
Goals	1. _____ 2. _____ 3. _____ 4. _____
Activities with Dog	1. _____ 2. _____ 3. _____ 4. _____
Goals Achieved	Goal #1: Yes / No Goal #2: Yes / No Goal #3: Yes / No Goal #4: Yes / No
Relaxation Exercise	Yes / No If yes, which one? _____
Fear Scale	Beginning:_____ Middle:_____ End: _____
Next Session	Date: _____ Plan: _____ _____ _____

"I am brave with dogs!"

This certificate hereby declares that

_____

gets a gold star for:

❏ Being near a dog
❏ Petting a dog
❏ Brushing a dog
❏ Giving a dog a treat
❏ Shaking a dog's paw
❏ Walking a dog

...but mostly for being
BRAVE AND KIND!

_____

(adult signature)

Resources

Please note at the time of printing this list was current. This is only a small sample of all the wonderful information out there.

Helpful Websites to Learn More About Dogs

- ❑ https://aspca.org
- ❑ https://www.akc.org/expert-advice/advice/how-to-read-dog-body-language/
- ❑ https://www.doggiedrawings.net/freeposters
- ❑ https://bestfriends.org/resources/dog-body-language
- ❑ www.drsophiayin.com
- ❑ www.doggonesafe.com
- ❑ https://kids-n-k9s.com/ - Lesley Zoromski has developed a sticker activity to help children learn about safety around dogs called "Stop, Look and Paws" which is available on this website.

To Discover Calming and Mindfulness Techniques

- ❑ https://www.mindful.org/
- ❑ https://www.headspace.com/meditation/kids
- ❑ www.stopbreathethink.com/kids/

To Learn More About the Human Animal Bond

- ❑ https://teenkidsnews.com
- ❑ www.avma.org
- ❑ https://www.uclahealth.org/pac/animal-assisted-therapy

❑ https://habri.org/ (Human Animal Bond Research Institute)
❑ https://www.americanhumane.org/

App for Your Phone

The **Dog Decoder App** by Dog Trainer Jill Breitner has dog poses to help you "decode" what a dog is feeling and communicating.

BOOKS FOR CHILDREN

About Dogs, Pet Care, and Safety around Dogs

❑ May I Pet Your Dog? by Stephanie Calmenson
❑ Dog Training for Kids: Fun and Easy Ways to Care for Your Furry Friend, by Vanessa Estrada Marin
❑ Are You Ready for Me? by Claire Buchwald
❑ Inside of a Dog -- Young Readers Edition: What Dogs See, Smell, and Know, by Alexandra Horowitz and Sean Vidal Edgerton
❑ One Incredible Dog!: Lady, by Chris Williams

To Establish an Open Mindset and "Can Do" Attitude in Kids

Laurie Wright has a series of 8 short books in her Mindful Mantras series. They are illustrated by Ana Santos and my two favorites are I Will Try and I Can Do It.

❑ My Strong Mind: A Story About Developing Mental Strength (Positive Mindset series), by Niels van Hove

Meditation and Mindfulness

❑ Listening to My Body: A guide to helping kids understand the connection between their sensations (what the heck are those?) and feelings so that they can get better at figuring out what they need, by Gabi Garcia and Ying Hui Tan
❑ Peaceful Piggy Meditation, by Kerry Lee MacLean

- ❏ Paint a Double Rainbow: 40 Mindfulness Activities for Kids and Their Grown-Ups to Feel Calm, Focused, and Happy, by Sally Arnold

To Help Children Cope with Anxiety and Fear

- ❏ What to Do When You Worry Too Much: A Kid's Guide to Overcoming Anxiety (What-to-Do Guides for Kids), by Dawn Huebner
- ❏ I Can Be Brave: Overcoming Fear, Finding Confidence, and Asserting Yourself (The Safe Child, Happy Parent Series), by Holde Kreul

BOOKS FOR ADULTS

About Dogs and Dog Behavior

- ❏ The Canine Good Citizen: Every Dog Can Be One, by Jack Volhard and Wendy Volhard
- ❏ A Dog Who's Always Welcome: Assistance and Therapy Dog Trainers Teach You How to Socialize and Train Your Companion Dog Hardcover, by Lorie Long
- ❏ Inside of a Dog: What Dogs See, Smell, and Know, by Alexandra Horowitz
- ❏ It's Me or the Dog – How to have the Perfect Pet, by Victoria Stilwell
- ❏ Please Don't Bite the Baby (and Please Don't Chase the Dogs), by Lisa J. Edwards

About the Human-Animal Bond

- ❏ The Healing Power of Pets, by Dr. Marty Becker with Danelle Morton
- ❏ Above All, Be Kind – Raising a Humane Child in Challenging Times, by Zoe Weil

About Anxiety in Children

- Helping Your Anxious Child, by Ronald M. Rapee, Ann Wignall, Susan H. Spence, Vanessa Cobham, and Heidi Lyneham
- The Worried Child, by Paul Foxman, Ph.D

The OFOD Protocol requires a well-trained and calm dog to put the protocol into practice. Many people will be able to borrow a friend or relative's dog but if that is not possible you may be able to find a therapy dog/handler team to assist you.

To Find Therapy Dogs:

- ❑ https://www.therapydogs.com/ (Alliance of Therapy Dogs)
- ❑ https://www.tdi-dog.org (Therapy Dogs International)
- ❑ https://petpartners.org

Local communities, animal shelters, and humane societies often have their own therapy dog programs as well.

Professional Dog Trainers are also good resources and may have access to well-behaved dogs to help you put the protocol into practice.

- ❑ https://www.ccpdt.org (Certification for Professional Dog Trainers)
- ❑ https://apdt.com (Association of Professional Dog Trainers)
- ❑ https://m.iaabc.org (International Association of Animal Behavior Consultants)

To find professional therapists who may be willing to assist you with the protocol and/or help your child with anxiety

When initially looking for a professional therapist for your child, it is advised to ask your child's pediatrician for a recommendation of a licensed mental health counselor, social worker or psychologist.

❑ https://www.psychologytoday.com/us/therapists
❑ https://www.helppro.com
❑ Goodtherapy.org

Endnotes

1 According to Statista, a total of about 89.7 million dogs lived as pets in households in the United States in 2017. Source: https://www.statista.com/statistics/198100/dogs-in-the-united-states-since-2000/

2 Paul Foxman, Ph.D., The Clinician's Guide to Anxiety Disorders in Kids and Teens, p. 88

3 U.S. National Library of Medicine, https://medlineplus.gov/ency/article/002059.htm?utm_source=email&utm_medium=share&utm_campaign=mplus_share

4 Source: Psychologytoday.com, Understanding Children's Emotions: Pride and Joy, posted on 5/14/12

5 http://healthland.time.com/2011/01/24/the-key-to-health-wealth-and-success-self-control/

6 http://www.pethealthcouncil.co.uk

7 Carol S. Dweck, Ph.D., Mindset, The New Psychology of Success, p.7, 2016 Ballantine Books

8 Quote taken from the Psychology Today website, Choosing Positive Words Improves Mindset and Performance by Christopher Bergland, published on December 7, 2012.

9 https://www.petmd.com/blogs/fullyvetted/2013/april/why-do-dogs-yawn-30190

10 https://www.hecoalition.org/what-is-humane-education.html

11 https://www.thefamilydog.com/stop-the-77/

12 https://kids-n-k9s.com/

13 https://doggonesafe.com/why_dogs_bite

14 http://www.robinkbennett.com/2013/08/19/why-supervising-dogs-and-kids-doesnt-work/

15 https://www.aspca.org/pet-care/dog-care/common-dog-behavior-issues/barking

16 https://www.dogster.com/lifestyle/dogs-affection-humans-dog-behavior-body-language

17 Source: https://www.akc.org/expert-advice/training/are-they-playing-or-fighting/

18 https://www.doggonesafe.com/Signs_of_a_Happy_Dog

19 Source: https://humaneeducation.org/blog/2015/humane-education-children-form-"opinions-nonhuman-animals-early/

20 Source: https://www.helpguide.org/articles/mental-health/mood-boosting-power-of-dogs.htm/

Made in United States
North Haven, CT
23 June 2024

53955653R00115